The End Of History

A Commentary On The Warrior's Way:
A System Of Knowledge First Reported In The Books Of Carlos Castaneda

By James L. Desper Jr.

THIRD ATTENTION PUBLISHING

NEW YORK LONDON PARIS CAIRO BEIJING

© 2012 James L. Desper, Jr.

THIRD ATTENTION PUBLISHING

All Rights Reserved

thejldj@yahoo.com

For more on the Warrior's Way, contact us at the above e-mail address

For the young

Contents

Introduction......Pg. 7
1. The Spirit......Pg. 8
2. The Third Attention......Pg. 11
3. Conserving Energy......Pg. 18
4. *Stalking* Ourselves......Pg. 29
5. *Dreaming*......Pg. 32
6. No Longer a Piece of Meat......Pg. 44
7. The 1960's......Pg. 48
8. The Authenticity of Castaneda's Reportage......Pg. 50
9. The Transition to the Third Attention......Pg. 53
10. Psychoactive Plants and the Warrior's Way......Pg. 56
11. Energy, Creativity and Wellness......Pg. 59
12. The Conditions of Modern Life......Pg. 63
13. The Misunderstanding......Pg. 65
14. The Flyers......Pg. 67
15. The Sexual Obsession......Pg. 69
16. Evil......Pg. 72
17. The Beginnings of the Warrior's Way......Pg. 75
18. The Inorganic Beings......Pg. 78
19. Why the Warrior's Way? And Why Now?......Pg. 84
20. The Life of Don Juan Matus......Pg. 87
21. A Summary of Practical Applications of the Warrior's Way......Pg. 111
22. The Moment of Revelation......Pg. 117

Appendices

Author's Notes......Pg. 118
A Note on Terminology......Pg. 119
A Brief Reader's Guide to Carlos Castaneda's Books......Pg. 121
Carlos Castaneda - Three Pronged Nagual?......Pg. 124
The Return of the Nagual Woman......Pg. 130
The Blue Scout......Pg. 138

**Debunking De Mille......Pg. 141
Source Notes......Pg. 170
Bibliography......Pg. 193**

Introduction

The universe and everything in it is composed of energy. What we call mass, or matter, is energy that we perceive in a different form. All energy either has awareness or it does not. Inanimate energy has a container, a shell, but no awareness. When the human body is perceived as pure energy, it is seen as a luminous egg-shaped shell roughly the size of the body with its arms outstretched. A bright spot on the luminous shell is the connection between the energy of the universe and the energy of the luminous shell, our human energy. The position of that point of contact on the luminous energy shell determines all perception and is called by warriors the assemblage point, the point where perception is assembled. This position can be altered by willing its movement, thus changing the content of our perception. Sometimes the position of the assemblage point shifts slightly; these shifts determine our moods, feelings and mode of living.

Warriors have identified over 600 positions on our luminous energy shell at which the assemblage point can assemble for perception entirely new worlds as real and objective as the one we are currently capable of perceiving. But the ultimate goal of a warrior is to move the assemblage point in such a way as to free our energy from the boundaries of the luminous energy shell and to merge it with the universe at large so that we retain our awareness in a form that will last as long as the Earth itself lasts. This is called entering the Third Attention of awareness. One of its defining features is a great dome of unimaginable size where all those who have reached the Third Attention can meet.

But willing the movement of the assemblage point to reach the Third Attention requires a higher level of personal energy than we have available in our usual mode of living. To conserve sufficient energy to will the movement of the assemblage point, the seers of the past created a new way of life, the Warrior's Way.

1. The Spirit

The universe is an immeasurable collection of energy fields that look like strands of light. These energy fields are called the Eagle's emanations because they come from a source of infinite magnitude that warriors call the Eagle. The force that powers the Eagle's emanations is called intent, the abstract, or the spirit.

All positive developments that occur in the life of a warrior are gifts of the spirit. When a warrior follows the recommendations of the Warrior's Way to increase her energy level, she entices the spirit forward. The spirit responds to a warrior's desire to clean her connecting link to the spirit so that she can express the intent of the spirit in every act, in every moment. At a certain point, a warrior reaches the stage of her development where her command becomes the spirit's command. This should never be taken to mean that a warrior controls the spirit, but that the warrior's connecting link to the spirit is strong enough that she can take direct action to express the intent of the spirit in pragmatic terms.

"For a warrior, the spirit is an abstract simply because he knows it without words or even thoughts. It's an abstract because he can't conceive what the spirit is. Yet without the slightest chance or desire to understand it, a warrior handles the spirit. He recognizes it, beckons it, entices it, becomes familiar with it, and expresses it with his acts. Consider this. It was not the act of meeting me that mattered to you. The day I met you, you met the abstract. But since you couldn't talk about it, you didn't notice it. Warriors meet the abstract without thinking about it or seeing it or touching it or feeling its presence." (8,2,58-59)

Impeccable men and women do not need a teacher to guide them. Their pure desire to know and express the spirit's intent is all that is required. But it is extremely important to know that once a warrior's assemblage point is loosened from its usual position, it can shift without warning, plunging a warrior into the depths of depression or to the heights of elation. It is one of a warrior's tasks to be on the lookout for these extreme shifts and to know that these shifts are temporary phenomena that signal a movement of the assemblage point to a position that brings them closer to knowing the spirit's intent. They are a sign of progress.

"Any movement of the assemblage point is like dying. Everything in us gets disconnected, then reconnected again to a source of much greater power. That amplification of energy is felt as a killing anxiety. [Castaneda asks, "What am I to do when this happens?"] Nothing. Just wait. The outburst of energy will pass. What's dangerous is not knowing what is happening to you. Once you know, there is no real danger." (8,4,169)

The spirit animates, gives life to the universe through the Eagle's emanations. The emanations can be classified into three groups–the known, the unknown and the unknowable. We are all familiar with the emanations that we perceive as our daily world. These are the known. A much larger group of emanations is the unknown, which when accessed by our perception can become the known because our perception can translate them into a landscape, a universe that we can perceive in an organized fashion. The largest group of emanations by far is the unknowable. When a warrior's assemblage point accesses the unknown he feels excited, adventurous, and has a strong sense of daring. But when he happens across the unknowable, a warrior feels drained, enervated and confused. Trying to perceive the unknowable quickly drains a warrior's energy and can result in his death. So it is vitally important that the warrior move his assemblage point back to a position he is familiar with as quickly as possible.

A warrior trusts his personal power whether it is great or small. Since a warrior is not acting out of self-importance but to further the intent of the spirit, such trust is invested in the spirit itself. One common activity that saps our personal power is the accumulation of possessions. Instead of focusing energy on the spirit, we are too often obsessed with the quantity and safety of our personal possessions. They are a dead weight that drags us back into the predator's mind. The predator believes that his possessions will ensure his safety and give him an advantage over those he sees as his competitors. But there is no safety and no security in this world. The only thing we can possess is our personal energy. And the concern that one has with their personal possessions saps that energy.

It is recommended that a warrior should possess only the items that are necessary to carry on his profession and a very few select items that give him great peace and pleasure. These a warrior uses as shields to protect himself, to distract him from the often frightening aspects of the warrior's path. They help to assure the return of a warrior's assemblage point to its usual position in the aftermath of the sometimes violent and disorienting shifts of the assemblage point that can occur while pursuing the warrior's path.

"I said that a warrior selects the items that make his world. He selects deliberately, for every item he chooses is a shield that protects him from the onslaughts of the forces he is striving to use. For that purpose you must have a selected number of things that give you great peace and pleasure, things you can deliberately use to take your thoughts from your fright... The things a warrior selects to make his shields are the items of a path with heart." (2,14,260-262)

Don Juan stated that there is no way to pray to the spirit because the human part of the spirit is too small to affect the whole. Our only available course of action is to strive to express the intent of the spirit. Therefore a warrior deals with the spirit exclusively in the realm of the abstract, the impersonal. The spirit can only assist the warrior in the pursuit of the knowledge that will help him to express the intent of the spirit.

We must all acquiesce to the intent of the spirit, either willingly or unwillingly. The advantage that warriors have is to realize the inevitability of that acquiescence and to act accordingly.

2. The Third Attention

The end of history is upon us. A time when all people who choose to do so will meet at the great dome of the Third Attention. Not as disembodied spirits of the dead, but as living awareness. Our bodies not left to decay in this world, but transformed into pure energy capable of astounding, unthinkable feats. It means the end of the physical pleasures of the body, but not of the feelings that give us hope and joy, that truly sustain us in this world, as they shall in the Third Attention. It is the will, the intent of the spirit that this vast transformation should occur, lest our continued presence damage and destroy this world that is also a manifestation of the spirit's intent.

"For warriors, when the act of unification [entering the third attention] takes place, there is no corpse. There is no decay. Their bodies in their entirety have been turned into energy, energy possessing awareness... (12,13,192)

The transition to the Third Attention changes our energy mass to one that is sustainable for an almost infinite duration. When a warrior achieves this level of sustainability the concept of time is irrelevant. Time is only useful as a means of measuring changes in energy level. We see things around us grow and wither. But if nothing ever changes, time means nothing. A second, a day, a year or a millennium are all the same to a warrior if his energy level remains the same.

"I'm convinced that under their [men of knowledge] direction, the populations of entire cities went into other worlds and never came back." (7,1,18-19)

When we attain the Third Attention we will meet others who will acquaint us with tales of ancient civilizations now unknown to us. Civilizations perhaps far more advanced than our own, from eons before, who finally discovered that the Third Attention is the ultimate, final evolution and destination of humanity. Civilizations that have repeatedly chosen to sustain their awareness for as long as the Earth itself shall live, rather that letting their awareness die with the physical body in this world. We will find that the change about to occur has happened countless times before, and will happen countless times again. But we will join those who have witnessed these changes and so much more with the power of perception available only to those who have reached the Third Attention.

When I say the end of history, I only mean the end of history for people this time around, so to speak. There will undoubtedly be small numbers of those who will remain in this world, by choice or ignorance of unfolding events, to continue the traditional cycle of life and death that we now know.

Our life in this world will end in fire. But not the fires of destruction, the fire from within.

To reach the Third Attention does not mean awareness that never ends. It means that we can sustain our awareness only so long as the Earth, the living being that shelters and sustains us now, shall live. Such is our present state of knowledge. Perhaps some of those who have reached the Third Attention will discover means to transfer our awareness to another being like the Earth that will shelter us if the Earth should lose all energy and die. But this is mere speculation. To keep our awareness for the millions and perhaps billions of years of life that the Earth has left is far superior to the short life span that people now experience. When we reach the Third Attention we become pure energy, pure awareness, a being capable of perception unthinkable for us in our present state of awareness.

"This [the third attention] is in no way immortality. It is merely the entrance into an evolutionary process, using the only medium for evolution that man has at his disposal: awareness. The warriors of my lineage were convinced that man could not evolve biologically any further; therefore, they considered man's awareness to be the only medium for evolution. At the moment of leaving this world, warriors are not annihilated by death, but are transformed into a specialized type of [independent] *inorganic being*: a being that has awareness, but not an organism. To be transformed into an inorganic being was evolution for them, and it meant that a new, indescribable type of awareness was lent to them, an awareness that would last for veritably millions of years, but which would also someday have to be returned to the giver: the Eagle." (10,5,104)

Warriors have discovered that the reason for life, the goal of life, is the enhancement of awareness. As all living things advance through the stages of life, their awareness is enriched through experience. But at the moment of death, the spirit collects and assimilates the awareness of all living creatures. This is why that, at the moment of death, our life flashes before our eyes.
The agent of the spirit that collects awareness is called by warriors the Eagle. Warriors refer to the awareness collected by the Eagle as the Eagle's food, but that is merely a way of talking about a phenomenon that we have no real way of understanding.

It is only from the Eagle's actions that a seer can tell what it wants. The Eagle, although it is not moved by the circumstances of any living thing, has granted a gift to each of those beings. In its own way and right, any one of them, if it so desires, has the power to keep the flame of awareness, the power to disobey the summons to die and be consumed. Every living thing has been granted the power, if it so desires, to seek an opening to freedom and to go through it. It is evident to the seer who sees the opening, and the creatures that go through it, that the Eagle has granted that gift in order to perpetuate awareness. (6,13,177)

Our awareness will be food for the Eagle eventually, but a warrior intends to put off that eventuality for as long as possible. The spirit intends this so that a warrior's awareness is richer food for the Eagle when it is eventually consumed.

But it is human nature to always seek a way out, an escape hatch, to put off that which we'd rather not face. Perhaps the Third Attention will only be a stepping stone to other, even more awesome realms of awareness to follow. But for now it is our task to reach for the inconceivable, the sublime, the Third Attention.

It is time to lead. Time to begin the work of building a bridge to the world of warriors, and thus to the Third Attention. There are those who have made the mistake of investing their hopes and dreams into one man, Castaneda, instead of in the Warrior's Way, where such thoughts should properly reside. The indulgence in physical pleasures which claimed his life and awareness does not have to take ours. The messenger died but the message lives on. The Warrior's Way means light in the gathering darkness, hope and joy in the face of growing cynicism, violence and despair. We can choose to be happy or to be miserable, but we can only choose once. It is time to lead.

Warriors speak of the warrior's way as a magical, mysterious bird which has paused in its flight for a moment in order to give man hope and purpose; that warriors live under the wing of that bird, which they call the bird of wisdom, the bird of freedom; that they nourish it with their dedication and impeccability. Warriors know the flight of the bird of freedom is always a straight line, since it has no way of making a loop, no way of circling back and returning; and that the bird of freedom could do only two things, take warriors along, or leave them behind. Warriors should not forget, even for an instant, that the bird of freedom has very little patience with indecision, and when it flies away, it never returns. (8,1,42-44)

"We choose only once. We choose either to be warriors or to be ordinary men. A second choice does not exist. Not on this earth. (5,5,271)

For those who begin this movement to total freedom, the task ahead is immense and daunting. It will require an extraordinary depth of character, extreme courage, an iron determination and absolute, total detachment. Not only will those in the vanguard have to live the tenets of the Warrior's Way, they will also have to deal with a skeptical and sometimes hostile reaction from the public and their friends and family. They will have to be fully functional warriors in total control of the movement of the assemblage point. Fortunately, they will not have to train the masses of people to achieve their level of control and discipline. Those who they will lead to freedom need only to be able to move their assemblage points away from their customary positions and to have recapitulated their lives. Then they can be swept up in the energy of the moment of transition sparked by the warriors who lead them.

Remaining in the orbit of friends and family is a much bigger task than it seems because they keep a warrior's assemblage point locked in its usual position. Traditionally an apprentice warrior is ordered to leave his friends and family so that his assemblage point can more easily lose its rigidity. But the new warriors will not necessarily have that option, making the task of moving the assemblage point that much more difficult. An analogous situation would be such as when a soldier enlists in the armed forces. A new recruit is always sent to a distant location, far from friends and family in order for his training to give him the mindset of a soldier —or in warrior's terms, a new position of the assemblage point.

To effectively lead others we must set an example. One way of doing this is a method called "visible personality." Neatness of appearance, good posture, strength, physical fitness, kindness, warmth, humor and tolerance inspire admiration and emulation in others. They will ask themselves, "What's his secret? What is he doing that I'm not? Does he know something that I don't?" Eventually people will stop you to ask of these things and your response will be rapidly spread to countless others through the best advertising of all, word of mouth. We have to become salesmen for the spirit. As crass as that sounds, it probably is the most accurate description of the task ahead to spread the Warrior's Way across the globe. We'll never use a hard sell, but by setting an example that others will wish to follow.

And others, when they see how hard it is to compete with warriors in the workplace and marketplace, will want to know why this is so and learn about the Warrior's Way to improve their own position. Perhaps their motives will be self-important at the beginning, but when they are immersed in the Warrior's Way many of them will change. Those who don't will make no progress anyway. Some of those who become jealous of warriors may spread vicious lies about the Warrior's Way. Or some may feel so insecure that they will make ignorant comparisons designed to discredit a warrior and his beliefs. It must be made clear that the Warrior's Way is a mechanism of persuasion, not of coercion.

"Turn everything into what it really is: the abstract, the spirit... There is no witchcraft, no evil, no devil. There is only perception." (8,6,231)

Words have magical power. They set events in motion. They awaken intent, the spirit. Thus the more that we write and speak of the Warrior's Way and the Third Attention, the more momentum we will build. The basic concepts of the Warrior's Way must be drilled into us through constant repetition. This is the way our parents and others taught us to perceive this world, and how that we will teach ourselves to perceive the world of warriors.

"Repeat to yourself incessantly that the hinge of the warrior's way is the mystery of the assemblage point. If you repeat this to yourself long enough, some unseen force takes over and makes the appropriate changes in you." (9,9,172)

But words alone are not nearly enough. The Warrior's Way is a philosophy of action. Thus we must take the necessary steps to conserve enough energy to move our assemblage points. And to practice controlling that movement through the exercises of *dreaming* and *stalking* ourselves.

"You should know by now that a man of knowledge lives by acting, not by thinking about acting, nor by thinking about what he will think when he has finished acting." (2,5,106-107)

The final frontier is where it has always been, within ourselves. It is within our power to see far horizons, distant worlds of dreams and separate realities, human possibilities undreamt-of in an ancient past still re-enacted daily. Our old ways of perceiving the world threaten our survival, so they must go. In their place, a new discipline, a new firmness, a willingness to meet new challenges free of the dead weight of self-concern. To experience life to its ultimate possibility; to extend human awareness until the Earth itself will die. Don Juan called it "the somersault of thought into the inconceivable." It is time to expand our imaginations and seize the moment, seize our last chance. It is no error that the Warrior's Way is emerging now. It is the world's way of avoiding the messy end we are driving ourselves to. It is the spirit's gift to us and to itself.

"Freedom is the Eagle's gift to man. Unfortunately, very few men realize that all we need, in order to accept such a magnificent gift, is to have sufficient energy." (7,Epilogue,295)

3. Conserving Energy

Human beings are born with a finite supply of energy, some with more than others. The amount of energy each person holds is different for everyone. Thus one can never know exactly when we might run out completely, and die. I think of our energy supply as a spring fed by an underground lake. The spring may get temporarily depleted, but will refill as long as the lake itself has not been emptied.

"Death is always waiting, and when the warrior's power wanes death simply taps him." (3,12,167)

The human activity that uses up most of our energy, that keeps our awareness focused totally on ourselves and not on the spirit, is self-importance. Our self-importance forces us to spend our entire lives feeling offended by other people, worrying what other people think of us, thinking about how to manipulate other people for our own ends or congratulating ourselves for being so happy and content. What maintains our self-importance is our internal dialogue, our thoughts. This internal dialogue can be stopped through an act of the warrior's will, thus stopping self-importance in its tracks and saving tremendous amounts of energy to be used to move the assemblage point.

"Self-importance is our greatest enemy. Think about it—what weakens us is feeling offended by the deeds and misdeeds of our fellow men. Our self-importance requires that we spend most of our lives offended by someone. The new seers recommended that every effort should be made to eradicate self-importance from the lives of warriors. I have followed that recommendation, and much of my endeavors with you has been geared to show you that without self-importance we are invulnerable." (7,1,26)

The internal dialogue also keeps our assemblage points fixed in one position by forcing us to tell ourselves over and over that the world is exactly as we believe it to be and that no other method of perceiving the world is possible. Our parents and others implanted this internal dialogue in us during our early childhood, when we were being taught to perceive the world as they perceive it. So a warrior strives to end this self-defeating internal dialogue that ends in death and replace it with one that focuses on our connecting link to the spirit and how to perceive the spirit directly without the intervention of thought.

"You think and talk too much. You must stop talking to yourself. You talk to yourself too much. You're not unique at that. Every one of us does that. We carry on an internal talk. We talk about our world. In fact we maintain our world with our internal talk. Whenever we finish talking to ourselves the world is always as it should be. We renew it, we kindle it with life, we uphold it with our internal talk. Not only that, but we also choose our paths as we talk to ourselves. Thus we repeat the same choices over and over until the day that we die, because we keep on repeating the same internal talk over and over until the day we die. A warrior is aware of this and strives to stop his talking." (2,14,263)

One method that don Juan recommended for shutting off the internal dialogue is "the right way of walking." With the fingers on both hands slightly curled, one walks for long distances with the eyes slightly crossed so they are out of focus and looking a little above the horizon. The combination of the concentration required to keep the fingers curled and the flood of information from the eyes (since they are not focused on any one item but are seeing everything in the visual range) overwhelms the senses and shuts down the internal dialogue.

We stop talking to ourselves the same way that we started, with an act of will. A warrior intends it and then her command becomes the spirit's command.

A warrior accumulates inner silence (a different amount for every warrior) until she reaches a crucial threshold when the world stops being that which was described since birth. When this point is reached the tableau in front of her, whatever it may be, beginning with a small brushstroke of color, starts to turn lavender. The lavender deepens until a dot of pomegranate red emerges and out of that comes images, thoughts or written words which are a result of reaching silent knowledge, which is direct contact with the spirit. Inner silence is a doorway to silent knowledge and *dreaming*, both of which will be discussed in detail later.

Another method of saving vast amounts of energy is to conserve our sexual energy. Engaging in sexual activity by oneself or with others is one of the fastest ways to deplete our energy resources. This is not so obvious when one is young and vigorous but becomes clearer as one ages and our overall energy diminishes. But even for the young, sex depresses the immune system, making one more vulnerable to illness. It takes the edge off of intellectual acuity. It also takes the edge off of the physical performance of the body in any task in which it might be engaged. And the older the individual, the more pronounced the effect. We must not forget that the amount of energy we have at our command varies widely from person to person, even for the young. So sexual activity can be disastrous at any age. Death taps us when we run out of energy, old or young.

Conserving our sexual energy will provide an immediate and powerful energy boost, but one must be careful not to let that extra energy be used for self-importance. Stopping sexual activity is much easier than killing self-importance, which is every warrior's most deadly enemy. One rather contradictory result of conserving sexual energy is that it makes us much more attractive to the opposite sex. It gives the practitioner an electric aura that is almost irresistible. People unconsciously sense stored sexual energy and react with respect, affection and even fear and anger. Those who sense the presence of strong sexual energy in those they feel could be rivals for the attention of the opposite sex may react with anger and even physical or psychological violence. Sexual attractiveness is usually judged by physical beauty or strength. But all too often, those who carry these attributes are so relentlessly praised and pursued by others that they become poisoned by their own vanity and self-importance. This effect caused one of the members of don Juan's warriors party, Florinda, to state that where one finds the most beautiful, one will also find the most wretched.

It is important to remember that we must never feel as if we are denying ourselves something when we utilize the tools for saving energy that the Warrior's Way offers. That feeling of missing out on something or losing something is a self-important indulgence and should be avoided at all costs. We are finding our power, our maximum energy, our absolute limit of perception. This is a gift of the spirit and something to be celebrated and praised. So the work should be done joyfully or not at all. Where some see sacrifice, a warrior sees opportunity, and grabs it.

"Denying yourself is an indulgence and I don't recommend anything of the kind. The indulgence of denying is by far the worst; it forces us to believe we are doing great things, when in effect we are only fixed within ourselves." (2,10,179)

We can retrieve vast amounts of energy consumed during our past interactions with other people through the use of the recapitulation. Recapitulation has been described as expelling foreign energy filaments or fragments left in our luminous energy shell from interactions with other people while we also retrieve our own personal energy lost in those interactions. To the logical mind it makes no sense that a simple breathing and memory exercise could accomplish this, but the gifts of the spirit and the Warrior's Way itself defy logic and are meant to astound, delight and enlighten us. They are not meant to cater to our preconceived, self-important notions of bookkeeping and logic.

Recapitulation begins with a single breath that serves to awaken intent, the spirit. With the chin over the right shoulder, we inhale as we turn the head until it is over the left shoulder. Then exhale while looking straight ahead. Then we begin with the chin over the right shoulder. We inhale as we turn the head until it is over the left shoulder. We exhale as we turn the head until it is over the right shoulder. The inhalations and exhalations should be done at the same pace as our normal breathing pattern.

As we breathe we recollect the interactions and events of our lives as completely as possible. First we recollect those events of our lives which stand out among all the others. We start with these because the strong emotions involved in these events make them stick out in our minds, and the stronger the emotions involved, the more energy we reclaim by recapitulating these events. We try to return to the scene of the event, to attempt as closely as possible to actually relive the event. The deeper into our recollection we go the more energy we reclaim.

After recollecting the most important events and interactions of our lives, we begin remembering our interactions with every person that we have ever met, from the most recent to those furthest in the past. We start with the most recent because those memories are the freshest and because as we recapitulate our power of recall becomes keener, making the memories of the past more vivid.

Then we begin recapitulating events and people that intent points out to us. This occurs when we enter into internal silence and memories pop into our minds seemingly at random. We recapitulate that event and then return to internal silence to await the next. After this series of recollections the recapitulation turns to the impersonal. These are events that the person recapitulating did not participate in, but has been affected by either directly or indirectly.

Aside from regaining lost energy, the recapitulation is vital because it gives the Eagle a facsimile, a replica of our memories, our experiences, our awareness. Only after giving the Eagle this copy, this replica, are we free to enter the Third Attention. The recapitulation is a substitute for the awareness that the Eagle usually reclaims at the moment of death. Therefore it must be as complete and as perfect a replica as possible.

As we progress in recapitulation we come to an event called the usher. The usher is a recollection so complete, so deep, so startling that we feel that we are actually reliving the event.

After this occurs, our power to remember becomes so strong that we relive the events being recalled from that point forward. Our assemblage point returns to the spot it was in when we experienced the event in question. This enables us to reclaim the maximum amount of energy while providing a more perfect replica of our awareness for the Eagle.

The Two Rounds of Recapitulation

Formality:
a) Events that stand out in our memory
b) List of people and events from the present into the past
c) Impersonal events that have affected the person recapitulating
Fluidity:
Random people and events (personal and impersonal) suggested by inner silence

To prepare for recapitulation we make a detailed list of the items included above under Formality. Then we seek out a location where we can be alone and recapitulate without the threat of interruption. This location must be as quiet as is possible. Ideally it will be a small, enclosed space that reduces visual and aural stimulation and distraction to a minimum. Sitting on a low chair or stool that raises the knees above the level of the hips is ideal.

As little as a few hours of effective recapitulation will provide a perceivable boost in one's personal energy. I can state this with confidence from my own personal experience. Recapitulation also aids in giving fluidity to the movement of the assemblage point by moving it back and forth from its usual position to the position it was in when one experienced the event being recapitulated.

Another method of managing one's personal energy is through the use of the magical passes, body movements designed to redistribute and control the energy contained in the luminous shell. Repetitious activities that we are prone to engage in can cause energy to be distributed unevenly, creating blockages that hinder the free movement of the assemblage point. Since the free movement of the assemblage point is a warrior's prime objective, the practice of using the magical passes to keep energy distributed properly throughout the luminous shell is vital to a warrior's goals.

"The natural tendency of human beings is to push energy away from the centers of vitality by worrying, by succumbing to the stress of everyday life. [This energy] gathers on the periphery of the *luminous ball*, sometimes to the point of making a thick, barklike deposit. The magical passes agitate the energy that has been accumulated in the *luminous ball* and return it to the physical body itself." (10,1,15)

The number and variety of magical passes sometimes overwhelms practitioners at the beginning. The focus should be on the movements that they remember, not on trying to remember and practice them all.

And it should go without saying, but let's make it clear anyway, that using alcohol, tobacco, drugs or other artificial stimulants such as caffeine damages the body and consumes extravagant amounts of vital energy.

When a warrior cut herself off from her self concern, her self-importance, she gains tremendous energy, energy which easily overcomes all obstacles. Human opposition melts away because they cannot possibly match the overwhelming energy of a warrior. Since they unconsciously know and respect (and even fear) such energy, they move out of the way. Because the warrior has stopped acting out of human, self-important motivation, but is acting for the spirit, seemingly random events conspire to smooth a warrior's path.

A warrior makes his own luck. He waits for the feeling, which most would call intuition, and then acts on it. Not for himself, but for the spirit. As this facility is used, it expands into what warriors call *seeing*, the ability to read the thoughts and intentions of others, to intuit the course of events as they unfold and the ability to see into the future. Reading the thoughts of others is a relatively easy task, since the internal dialogues of most people are simple, repetitious, and nearly universal. They are concerned with very few things. Thoughts of food, shelter, sex, money and status rule their world. So how they will react in any given situation is a matter of determining which of those few drives is operative and dominating at the moment. But a warrior never uses this knowledge to feel superior to, or better than, other people. That self-importance would lead a warrior to her destruction. Since a warrior acts exclusively to further the intent of the spirit, she is totally detached and does not waste one bit of energy on such useless judgments.

When a warrior truly begins *seeing*, she will begin to hear what don Juan called "the voice of *seeing*," a disembodied voice that tells the seer what's what. If the voice of *seeing* is absent, then a warrior is not truly *seeing*.

To trigger *seeing*, one must beckon intent. Don Juan called the eyes "the catchers of intent." The gaze is focused on the luminous shell at a point called "the point of the second attention." This is located approximately 18 inches in front of the midpoint between the stomach and the belly button and 4 inches to the right. The head remains facing straight ahead; only the eyes move to concentrate on the point of the second attention. To return to perceiving the world in the usual manner the gaze is placed on the body. By bringing the point of the second attention closer to the body it becomes easier to control. The method for accomplishing this task is to manipulate the point of the second attention with the fingers of both hands the same way a musician plays a harp.

Don Juan said that "warriors should never attempt *seeing* unless they are aided by *dreaming*." (See Ch. 5 - *Dreaming*) The assemblage point is moved from its usual position by stopping the internal dialogue. Whenever the assemblage point leaves its usual position we are technically asleep (but still retain our bodily awareness as if awake) and the assemblage point reaches what is called a *dreaming position*. After the assemblage point moves far enough away from its usual spot to a *dreaming position* we fixate it by intending that fixation and then beckon intent with the eyes by focusing on the point of the second attention to begin *seeing*.

Seeing eventually expands into a consistent ability to directly perceive energy as it flows in the universe, putting the warrior into direct contact with the spirit's intent. The next step in mankind's evolution begins with silence, internal silence.

"Silent knowledge is something that all of us have, something that has complete mastery, complete knowledge of everything. But it cannot think, therefore, it cannot speak of what it knows. Warriors believe that when man became aware that he knew, and wanted to be conscious of what he knew, he lost sight of what he knew. This silent knowledge, which you cannot describe, is, of course, *intent* - the spirit, the abstract. Man's error was to want to know it directly, the way he knew everyday life. The more he wanted, the more ephemeral it became. It means that man gave up silent knowledge for the world of reason. The more he clings to the world of reason, the more ephemeral *intent* becomes." (8,4,167)

Silent knowledge is our history, our heritage, our birthright. Before thoughts could be formed, words—a vocabulary—had to be established. Since ancient people had no words, they acted totally within the arena of silent knowledge. While the absence of thought does not automatically mean easy access to silent knowledge, it removes a major impediment, the internal dialogue. The most basic units of silent knowledge for early man were survival skills, what we refer to as instinct. But because ancient peoples were often subjected to extremes of hunger, fear and pain, their assemblage points were moved to positions from which they experienced extremes of altered perception. Many of these altered perceptions formed the basis for what we call spirituality. And that is why spirituality, mysticism, is our most basic feature, after survival skills.

Among every group of people are naguals, teachers who can move the assemblage point of those they come into contact with by their mere presence. These people are adept at moving their assemblage points to new positions and to positions they have experienced previously, and consequently, moving the assemblage points of others to the same position. This occurs only through the intervention of the spirit and without the intervention of conscious thought. That is why that don Juan at one point told Castaneda that when Carlos met him (don Juan), he met the spirit.

So it is probable that the earliest naguals were able to intuit the possibility of reaching the Third Attention and lead others to that possibility. Those able to reach the Third Attention will meet others whom we might call cavemen, but whose perceptual sophistication makes mankind's present mindset seem primitive and barbaric.

"I didn't know that I was storing power when I first began to learn the ways of a warrior. Just like you, I thought I wasn't doing anything in particular, but that was not so. Power has the peculiarity of being unnoticeable when it is being stored." (3,14,214)

The younger one is, the less noticeable it will be that one is conserving energy. For young people, the energy saved during recapitulation and practicing the magical passes may be unnoticeable, as might be that of losing self-importance. The energy saved from conserving sexual energy might be noticed only as a sense of intense frustration, until the day one has stored enough personal power to make the world change.

"You must wait patiently, knowing that you're waiting, and knowing what you're waiting for. That is the warrior's way. What makes us unhappy is to want. Yet if we could learn to cut our wants to nothing, the smallest thing we'd get would be a true gift. To be poor or wanting is only a thought; and so is to hate, or to be hungry, or to be in pain."(2,9,173)

Warriors are divided by talent and inclination into two groups - *dreamers* and *stalkers*. *Dreamers* are those who most efficiently conserve energy and learn to manipulate the position of the assemblage point through dreaming practices. *Stalkers* are those who accomplish the same goal, but concentrate more of their activity on the practice of *stalking* themselves. Every warrior should strive to practice both, but usually a warrior can make more efficient use of one than of the other. The point is to conserve enough energy to move the assemblage point. Some techniques work better for some than for others. If one thing is not working then you try something else.

"Anything is one of a million paths. Therefore you must always keep in mind that a path is only a path; if you feel you should not follow it, you must not stay with it under any conditions. To have such clarity you must lead a disciplined life. Only then will you know that any path is only a path, and there is no affront, to oneself or to others, in dropping it if that is what your heart tells you to do. But your decision to keep on the path or to leave it must be free of fear or ambition. I warn you. Look at every path closely and deliberately. Try it as many times as you think necessary. This question is one that only a very old man asks. My benefactor told me about it once when I was young, and my blood was too vigorous for me to understand it. Now I do understand it. I will tell you what it is: Does this path have a heart? All paths are the same: they lead nowhere. They are paths going through the bush, or into the bush. In my own life I could say I have traversed long, long paths, but I am not anywhere. My benefactor's question has meaning now. Does this path have a heart? If it does, the path is good; if it doesn't, it is of no use. Both paths lead nowhere; but one has a heart, the other doesn't. One makes for a joyful journey; as long as you follow it, you are one with it. The other will make you curse your life. One makes you strong; the other weakens you." (1,5,82)

If one is to succeed in anything, the success must come gently, with a great deal of effort but with no stress or obsession. (4,1,20-21)

4. *Stalking* Ourselves

Stalking ourselves is a way of moving the assemblage point slowly and steadily from the its usual position in our daily lives and maintaining that new position with all its quirks and new possibilities. It consists of practicing unusual, or unusually controlled, behavior. Any activity outside our normal behavior causes a slight shift in the assemblage point. A warrior *stalks* himself ruthlessly in order to maximize the movement of his assemblage point from its usual position. Once the assemblage point moves away from its usual position, a warrior is free to move it to relatively more distant positions from where it most often rests on the luminous energy shell.

Stalking ourselves is also a most effective method of stopping the deadening effects of ingrained and repetitious habits that lead to boredom and cynicism. Boredom and cynicism lead us to feel that we know all there is to know, so why bother with new ideas or attitudes. They are ways of feeling that we are always right, no matter how wrong we may be. They are pure, unvarnished self-importance —every warrior's deadliest enemy.

A *stalker* begins by accepting that life, the world, and the universe are mysteries that we will never comprehend. But as a part of everything, we are a mystery also. We could spend many lifetimes trying to unravel these mysteries and still only scratch the surface. This realization gives a warrior the humility to accept that since that there is no end to the mysteries that surround us, everything is equal. The mystery of being a plant, an animal or a rock is equal to the mystery of being human.

Since we are equal to even the most insignificant bug or germ, a warrior can never take herself seriously. She learns to laugh at herself, particularly at her endless capacity for the self-importance that we all share. She learns that she must *stalk* herself ruthlessly, cunningly, patiently and sweetly; but not with harshness, cruelty, negligence or foolishness. These are also required for her dealings with the self-importance of others. A *stalker* uses this strategy to be ruthless while being charming, to be cunning but nice, to be patient but always ready to act, to be sweet but to be firm and assertive.

Part of a *stalker's* strategy is to never enter an unfamiliar situation without investigating it in advance. A *stalker* does his homework so that he will know as much as possible about the new surroundings and people that he will encounter. He knows that superfluous possessions and relationships are a drain on his energy and retains only those which are absolutely necessary to continue his quest to know and express the intent of the spirit. He knows that any moment could be his last, so he strives to act in every moment with what warriors call controlled abandon—a fierce energy tempered by total control. A *stalker* knows that sometimes she will face situations that cannot at first be dealt with, so she retreats momentarily to formulate a new strategy. She is always ready to improvise. She knows that since her time in this world is too short for appreciating all its marvels she does not have a moment to waste, but she never hurries. And she knows that to effectively exert pressure on others she must remain outside of the concerns that press upon them. She acts behind the scenes, never pushing herself to the front.

A *stalker* knows that words have magical power. They set events in motion. They awaken intent, the spirit. But a *stalker* must phrase his words carefully to merely hint at the intended events to follow. To state his aims clearly at the onset would be to confront others directly, something that a warrior avoids in every situation. An excellent example of the technique was the nagual Julian's (don Juan's teacher) assertion that he would, in one stroke, show don Juan not only what the spirit was, but also how to define it. What he really intended to do, and did quite successfully, was to put don Juan into direct contact with the spirit and let that contact result in the free movement of don Juan's assemblage point.

The power of words to set events in motion has been demonstrated countless times in human history. One example that has repeated itself many times concerns those who predict the manner and timing of their own death with their prediction so often coming to fruition. They were not clairvoyant, they were merely ignorant of the power of words.

"Some warriors object to the term *stalking*, but the name came about because it entails surreptitious behavior. It's also called the art of stealth, but that term is equally unfortunate. We ourselves, because of our nonmilitant temperament, call it the art of controlled folly. You can call it anything you wish. We, however, will continue with the term *stalking* since it's so easy to say *stalker* and, as my benefactor used to say, so awkward to say *controlled folly maker*." (8,3,102)

5. *Dreaming*

The true meaning and function of sleep has always been a mystery to mankind. The only explanation offered is that we need to rest, and only the physical immobilization of sleep can provide that rest. Simple, logical, but so simplistic that it betrays our total ignorance.

We sleep to regain contact with our true selves, the being capable of astounding acts of perception, capable of visiting other worlds as real as the one we know and those created by our own intentions. Sleep is actually a respite from the hard work of keeping our assemblage point immobilized in one spot to perceive this world in a sustained manner. When we sleep we "awaken" to our true selves. That is why warriors say that the dream dreams the dreamer.

Even a person who sits or lies quietly all day, engaging in no physical activity, must still sleep. This shows that what tires us is merely being "awake". So we can only truly "rest" when the assemblage point is free to move. Modern medical techniques have shown that we can survive for years without being in our everyday waking state, but there is no drug or therapy that can substitute for sleep.

At this point it would be reasonable to ask, "If sleep and dreaming reveals our true nature, why don't we sleep more, or all the time?" And the answer is that we must procure food and shelter to sustain life and awareness. To do this we must be a member of a group that has learned to hold its assemblage point steady in order to perceive a world capable of providing what we need to survive.

Modern man's problem is to believe that the struggle for survival is all that there is to our consciousness. To ignore our need for food and shelter would be fatal, but to ignore our power to change and expand our awareness is equally fatal in the long run.

We dream from the moment we fall asleep until the moment we awaken. But we can only remember the dreams that have made the strongest impression on us, those that touch facets of our personality that are both known and unknown to us. They point out our inclinations, our obsessions, many of which we cannot admit even to ourselves.

We visit places that are solely the creation of our own personalities and also worlds that are as real as the one we inhabit in our daily lives. If we chose to "wake up" in one of those real worlds, we could remain there, if desired, for the rest of our lives. All *dreaming* is the result of a movement of the assemblage point to a certain position. There are at least six hundred real worlds that are positions of the assemblage point on our luminous energy shell.

Don Juan informed Castaneda at one point that "*dreaming* is a warrior's jet plane." Awareness can be used as a means of physical transportation. This occurs when the assemblage point is displaced to a position outside the luminous energy shell. Strong interest, desire or unbending intent - will - then drags the energy of the luminous being to the new location.

But ordinary dreams are not *dreaming*. *Dreaming* occurs when warriors are aware that they are *dreaming* and that they have the power to use the free movement of their assemblage point to engage in whatever activity that they desire.

Dreaming is used to train a warrior how to make drastic shifts, large movements of the assemblage point and control the results of such shifts. As such it is a vital part of every warrior's training.

The first step is to intend to remember to look at your hands while dreaming. Before letting sleep overtake you, stop your internal dialogue and then bring the image of yourself looking at your hands into your mind. Then think to yourself, "Look at your hands." It may take several tries before you succeed because of the mind's internal resistance to changes in its routine. You may even find yourself sunk into an unexplained sadness or depression because of your desire to set up *dreaming*. But forewarned is forearmed, so just shake it off and keep trying. Persistence will win out in the end.

When you succeed in remembering to look at your hands, then you should begin to focus your gaze on the other objects in your dream. Glance at them briefly and then return to your hands. When you return your gaze to your hands you renew the energy needed to sustain your *dreaming*. With practice you will be able to look at your surroundings for longer and longer periods. If the images begin to change as you look at them, return your gaze to your hands. When you have learned to sustain the sight of your surroundings without having to look at your hands, you are ready to go on to the next step.

Just as you intended to look at your hands, you must intend to move, to go to different locations you are already familiar with. While *dreaming*, intend yourself to go to a place you know well. One technique that will aid your success in this task is to have memorized in advance an object or feature at this location. If you can recall while *dreaming* the image of the object that you have memorized, you can go there.

After you have succeeded in beginning to learn to move, then you can start trying to control the timing of your travels while *dreaming*. Ideally your travel to the intended location will occur in real time, at the same time that your body is in your bed asleep. One trick to help in this pursuit is to place a friend, preferably of the opposite sex, at the location at the time you intend to go there. Your desire to succeed in meeting them strengthens your will and spurs you on.

The techniques of moving and controlling its timing are very difficult and require great persistence. But once you have learned them you will have created what warriors refer to as your energy body, an exact replica of the physical body that is made of pure energy. The energy body is capable of traveling to any location you desire in your intention or even in the intentions of others.

An exercise that it is important for a *dreamer* to practice is changing dreams. This will often happen in the course of *dreaming* without being intended. When one focuses the *dreaming* attention on an item or feature of that dream we are pulled into another dream in a different situation or landscape. What we are striving for is to change to a new dream in an orderly fashion without confusion or loss of control setting in. An alternate way of changing dreams is to "awaken" from one dream into another. But both methods have the same goal—to control (and get used to controlling) the movement of the assemblage point. By intending to change dreams we learn to move the assemblage point and by maintaining the new dream we learn to fixate the new position of the assemblage point.

Dreaming teaches a warrior how to make instantaneous shifts of the assemblage point; the same kind of instant shift that occurs when we awaken from a dream. But since one of a warrior's goals is to make the assemblage point move from its usual position to a new position, it is important for a *dreamer* to practice trying to be aware of falling asleep. This teaches us the feeling we get at the moment that the assemblage point moves from its usual position. Becoming familiar with this feeling is key to making the assemblage point move on command.

There are a couple of different cues that one can pick up on when the assemblage point begins to move. Some *dreamers* experience the sound of a loud crack like the sound of two pieces of lumber smacked flat against each other. It can sometimes be so loud as to return the *dreamer* to a waking state. Another cue is noticing when the internal dialogue turns into nonsensical gibberish in the moments before sleep takes over. A third cue is what I call the advent of automatic breathing. You notice that you are breathing in a steady rhythmic manner without consciously controlling it. We do this all the time in our usual waking state, of course, but "automatic breathing" comes with the feeling that one no longer has control over it.

The trick is to notice the cues but not to let them return you to the waking state by letting the smooth transition of the assemblage point away from its usual position continue. With practice one can learn to move the assemblage point back and forth between the positions of wakefulness and dreaming in full awareness.

With the control learned in *dreaming* a warrior can move the assemblage point from its usual position to a distant one in the blink of an eye and then take the body's energy mass along with it. The energy body reaches the new *dreaming* position (of the assemblage point) and then intends the body's energy mass to follow. The energy body is a scout that determines if the new position of the assemblage point is a position that the body's energy mass can tolerate, can survive, before bringing it along for the ride. For instance, the energy body can visit and experience the most recondite spots in the cosmos that the body itself could never tolerate. But with experience a *dreamer* learns to move the assemblage point to precise positions that enable the body's energy mass to follow instantly. These positions naturally include any spot in this world, but also in other worlds, other universes, in which humans live.

(At this point I hope that you, the reader, will indulge me in a brief digression - the possibility that some of the human race actually spends enough time, while dreaming, in other worlds to consider that we "live" in them as we do in this one. The new seers have informed us that time is perceived quite differently in some of the worlds that we can access through *dreaming*; a minute is more like an hour, a day or even a year in some of these worlds. But the position of the assemblage point reached when experiencing these worlds is so distant from its usual position that it is almost impossible for us to remember our experience when it returns to the position that allows us to perceive this world. Of course, saying that we "live" in those other worlds would be an overstatement since our bodily mass remains in this world while dreaming. Should the condition of "living" in another world be quantified by where the body's energy mass resides or how much "time" is spent there? My speculation about this subject was triggered by a dream in which I was visiting some friends who ran a shop in an outdoor marketplace. In my normal awareness I could not remember ever having met them or visiting that place previously; but in my dream I apologized for not having visited them for such a long time and felt that I knew them well. How much "time" have I spent there? Was it a world as real and verifiable as this one? That dream has never been repeated, or if it has, I cannot remember it.)

Dreams are an opening, an escape hatch if you will, into other worlds. Some of these worlds are as real as the one you experience now and can act on you, affect you just as this world does. It is vital to be able to tell the difference between an environment generated by an ordinary dream and the landscape of a real world that one has reached through *dreaming*. Warriors do this by intending to see energy in their dreams. One technique for seeing energy in dreams is to point at an object or person and shout, "I want to see energy!" (This technique worked for me in my *dreaming* practices) Another is to point at an object with the little finger on either hand. After a while one has only to focus attention on an item and you will see energy. If you are in an ordinary dream the item you are focused on will disappear or change into something else. If you are in a real world the item will glow from its real internal energy. In ordinary dreams items do not glow because they have no real energy; they do not generate energy.

Reaching a real world through *dreaming* can be as dangerous as being in our daily world can be. Those worlds are as predatory as this one is. A *dreamer* can appear to the inhabitants of that world as a strange and threatening being that might be dangerous and should be eliminated. If an unidentified creature was roaming the streets of your hometown, it would be killed or captured to eliminate the possible threat. *Dreamers* can be expected to be treated in a similar fashion if they suddenly appear in other real worlds. You should always be prepared to instantly will the movement of the assemblage point in order to change dreams by remembering items or locations from other dreams or remembering that you are dreaming and can awake from sleep to return to the world of daily life.

Dreamers enter into what is essentially a no man's land of awareness that is also inhabited by other living beings that have an awareness quite different from that of our own. The most common forms of alien awareness that dreamers encounter are scouts from the world of inorganic beings. Inorganic beings are energetic awareness that has no solidity in the way we understand it; but they have consciousness and can interact with us if they so desire. They exist primarily in their own separate world (at the moment of entering the Third Attention a warrior becomes an inorganic being that is independent of the inorganic beings under discussion at this point) but can project themselves into this world as if a film projector was capable of throwing three dimensional images onto a movie screen. They are beings of low energy that seek the high energy of *dreamers*. And so they send their scouts in search of that energy in order to transport it to their world to feed off it. Merely being in the presence of a dreamer "warms" them like being in bright sunshine on a cold day.

Don Juan said that soliciting the presence of scouts from the realm of the inorganic beings is a method of making them noticeable and then enabling a *dreamer* to follow them to their realm in order the absorb the energy of that universe. Visiting their realm gives dreamers an energetic boost that makes the movement of the assemblage point easier.

"*Dreaming* is sustaining the position where the assemblage point has shifted in dreams. This act creates a distinctive energy charge, which attracts their attention. It's like bait to a fish; they'll go for it. Warriors ... set bait for those beings and compel them to appear. With inorganic beings, the secret is not to fear them. And this must be done from the beginning. Through the channel of fear, they can follow us to the daily world, with disastrous results for us. Inorganic beings can be worse than a pest. Through fear they can easily drive us raving mad. The intent one has to send out to them has to be of power and abandon. In that intent one must encode the message 'I don't fear you. Come to see me. If you do, I'll welcome you. If you don't want to come, I'll miss you." With a message like this, they'll get so curious that they'll come for sure. The thing you must bear in mind from now on is that inorganic beings with their superb consciousness exert a tremendous pull over dreamers and can easily transport them into worlds beyond description." (9,3,45-49)

The first form of alien energy that a dreamer may experience is the *dreaming* emissary. *Dreamers* find that they are talking to themselves so incessantly that it becomes an annoyance. On closer inspection they discover that it is not their internal dialogue, but a voice outside themselves. At this early stage it can be stopped by saying aloud, "Stop it!" But as a warrior begins to deal with inorganic beings it returns in an obviously more noticeable form. It attempts to aid and guide *dreamers* by telling them facts that they already know or should already know. It is actually, however, a salesperson for the inorganic beings. It guides *dreamers* through the world of the inorganic beings while attempting to persuade them to live in that world. It can be stopped by voicing aloud, during *dreaming*, one's intent to no longer have it. At that point a warrior can strike a bargain with it to ensure that it will only speak when asked a question directly. This is actually a fabulous bonus, since the *dreaming* emissary can sometimes tell warriors facts they would have no way of knowing otherwise.

The danger of visiting the inorganic beings is that they will attempt to persuade *dreamers* to live with them for the rest of their lives. One of their selling points is that living with them will extend the dreamer's life and awareness for eons longer than the life they would have by remaining in our daily world. And that is true, but the price for such an extended awareness is our freedom. A *dreamer* becomes the slave of the inorganic beings by agreeing to live in their world. The trick is to visit their world a few times to absorb as much of their energy as possible but not to succumb to the promises of knowledge and power that would make *dreamers* their slaves.

"[The decision to live with the inorganic beings] is a superpersonal and final decision, a final decision made the instant you voice your desire to live in that world. In order to get you to voice that desire, the inorganic beings are going to cater to your most secret wishes. [Castaneda says, "This is really diabolical, don Juan."] You can say that again. But not just because of what you are thinking. For you, the diabolical part is the temptation to give in, especially when such great rewards are at stake. For me, the diabolical nature of the inorganic beings' realm is that it might very well be the only sanctuary *dreamers* have in a hostile universe. Not for me. I don't need props or railings. I know what I am. I am alone in a hostile universe, and I have learned to say, So be it!" (9,5,96)

Dreamers may encounter scouts from worlds that are far more dangerous than those from the inorganic being's world. In the beginning, to follow a scout to the world of the inorganic beings one must state one's intent out loud. And to live with them one must do the same. But there are other, more powerful scouts that will compel a *dreamer* to follow them if attention is focused on them for more than a split second. Traveling to their worlds may dissipate a *dreamer's* energy instantly and result in death. Or a *dreamer's* awareness (the position of the assemblage point) could be fixated in one position, making the perception of that world the only one possible. If an item or person (these scouts like to hide behind the dream images of our parents or friends) in your dream suddenly changes into a bright orange ball of energy that seems to sizzle, look away immediately.

A *dreamer* must be constantly vigilant; the practice of *dreaming* should be treated with the same caution one would exercise if going into a war zone. It is equally dangerous.

"The Nagual Elias (the Nagual Julian's teacher) had great respect for sexual energy. He believed it has been given to us so we can use it in *dreaming*. He believed *dreaming* had fallen into disuse because it can upset the precarious mental balance of susceptible people. I've taught you *dreaming* the same way he taught me. He taught me that while we dream the assemblage point moves very gently and naturally. Mental balance is nothing but the fixing of the assemblage point on the one spot we're accustomed to. If dreams make that point move, and *dreaming* is used to control that natural movement, and sexual energy is needed for *dreaming*, the result is sometimes disastrous when sexual energy is dissipated in sex instead of *dreaming*. Then *dreamers* move their assemblage points erratically and lose their minds. You are a *dreamer*. If you're not careful with your sexual energy, you might as well get used to the idea of erratic shifts of your assemblage point. Our sexual energy is what governs *dreaming*. The nagual Elias taught me–and I taught you–that you either make love with your sexual energy or you *dream* with it. There is no other way." (8,2,55-56)

Another possible pitfall *dreamers* face is this: The energy body must never come face to face with the physical body. The result is death. The most likely condition during which this could happen is when a *dreamer* finds herself looking at her sleeping body. This is a regular development for all *dreamers* so extreme caution must be exercised when it occurs.

There are several methods to enhance and facilitate the *dreaming* attention. One recommendation is to wear a headband while sleeping. There should be a strip across it that fits snugly on the top of the head. But one should only make it after having a vision of it while *dreaming*. Or its design can be suggested by a random event that occurs while awake. This should be a very distinctive and special incident that involves a natural phenomenon such as wind, clouds, water, the movements of flying birds, etc.

Another way to improve *dreaming* is to remember, while *dreaming*, to touch the tip of the tongue to the roof of the mouth. This helps to stabilize the position of the assemblage point so that *dreaming* becomes more like our ordinary waking state. One will have an almost equal feeling of control.

It is best to do *dreaming* late at night or very early in the morning. Our fellow human beings, some more than others, have the ability to subtly interfere with our energy configuration by concentrating their attention on us while they are awake. When they are asleep this interference is eliminated.

Concentrating attention on certain parts of the body can be a powerful aid to entering *dreaming* from a waking state. For men the area at the tip of the sternum/ the top of the belly; for women the womb. The energy for moving the energy body while *dreaming* can be enhanced for men by concentrating on the area an inch or so below the belly button. For women this energy again originates from the womb.

There are powerful energy centers in the human body on the inside of both of the upper thighs and on both sides of the lower part of the trunk. It is very desirable to bring these areas into close proximity to improve *dreaming* (and recapitulating). Consequently don Juan suggested that women sit with legs crossed and let themselves fall forward to bring these energy centers together. Men should sit with the soles of their feet touching each other while the thighs lie flat. They should then lean forward until the head rests on the feet. These positions require flexibility and discipline but can very definitely improve *dreaming*. Bringing these energy centers closer together is the reason that warriors are instructed to sit on a low chair or stool when recapitulating. This position brings the thighs in closer proximity to the lower trunk of the body while enabling one to sit upright for proper breathing and head movement.

"To venture into the world of warriors is not like learning to drive a car. To drive a car, you need manuals and instructions. To *dream*, you need to *intend* it." (10,5,119)

Don Juan described intending as "silent determination." Beyond that definition we end up in the paradoxical, contradictory territory we fall into when attempting to describe the parameters, the particulars, the boundaries of perception. Don Juan also said that to intend is "to wish without wishing, to do without doing." I like to think of it as the exercise of human will in a humble attempt to accede to the designs of the infinite, the spirit. What is important to remember is that our command becomes the Eagle's command when that command comes from an impeccable desire to clean our connecting link to the spirit.

Stages of Progression in *Dreaming*
1. Setting up *dreaming*–finding your hands in a dream to remind yourself that you are *dreaming*.
2. Learning to sustain the sight of any item in your dream.
3. Becoming aware that you are falling asleep.
4. Having a gigantically real dream.
5. Changing dreams in an orderly and precise manner by

either waking from one dream into another or by using items from one dream to trigger another dream.

6. Calling the inorganic beings to attract their attention and solicit their presence in your *dreaming*.

7. To isolate scouts from the inorganic beings' world and to follow them to their realm.

8. Refusing the temptation to stay in the inorganic beings' world, keeping yourself free for further progression.

9. Facing inorganic beings and wrestling with one in your normal awareness.

10. Seeing oneself asleep while *dreaming* and verifying that it is oneself at the moment of *dreaming*.

11. Learning to move the energy body.

12. *Seeing* energy with the energy body.

13. Using the energy of the inorganic beings' world to trigger a journey to unknown realms.

14. Using the energy body to travel to specific, concrete places in this world, in other worlds, or to places that exist only in the intent of others.

"Recapitulating and *dreaming* go hand in hand. As we regurgitate our lives, we get more and more airborne. The recapitulation sets free energy imprisoned within us, and without this liberated energy *dreaming* is not possible." (9,8,148)

"The recapitulation of our lives never ends, no matter how well we've done it once. The reason average people lack volition in their dreams is that they have never recapitulated and their lives are filled to capacity with heavily loaded emotions like memories, hopes, fears, et cetera, et cetera. Warriors, in contrast, are relatively free from heavy, binding, emotions, because of their recapitulation." (9,8,147-148)

6. No Longer a Piece of Meat

Warriors who have the energy to see the human body as pure energy, the luminous shell, have noted the fact that as it moves across the energy of the Earth it leaves a furrow in the Earth's energy, like a taproot dragging behind us. This shows that we are directly connected to the energy of the Earth. This energy sustains us. And it has been shown to be vital to our survival by the experiences of those who have severed their direct energetic connection to the Earth for long periods of time. I am speaking, of course, of astronauts who have remained in space for months at a time. Disconnected from the Earth's energy and unable to access a comparable energy source, the human body starts to consume itself. Scientists refer to this phenomenon as "the effects of zero gravity" (the phenomenon known as jet lag is a milder form of this energy depletion) and openly admit that, with the state of their present knowledge, any space travel of sufficient duration would be fatal to anyone who attempts it. This is the only reason that astronauts have not been sent to explore Mars, Venus or any other planet that would require years of space travel. Because science sees the human body as basically a piece of meat that, theoretically, they should be able to transport anywhere, their approach to solving this problem has produced no viable solution.

"Reason doesn't deal with man as energy. Reason deals with instruments that create energy, but it has never seriously occurred to reason that we are better than instruments: we are organisms that create energy. We are a bubble of energy." (7,7,119)

Because scientists are unaware of the body as pure energy and its energetic connection to the Earth, they have applied what I call the Piece of Meat Philosophy to all forms of human endeavor. A piece of meat cannot possibly experience visions, transcendence, spirituality or other realities. A piece of meat cannot possibly experience what we have traditionally called

"God". But the fact remains that every human being has the possibility of experiencing all of these. It is my fervent belief that many people experience what we have called "God" every day, but they have become so intimidated by the very real consequences of admitting such an experience that they keep it to themselves. And we all know exactly what they fear: ostracism, insult, isolation, violence and possibly even confinement in a mental institution await those bold enough to tell of their experience. Even the churches themselves will no longer admit the possibility of any individual directly experiencing "God".

This is quite a different mindset from that of the people who founded their religions in ancient times. Those men knew that every person is capable of experiencing "God". A personal relationship with "God" is the real goal that these people meant for those they led. A good example is Christianity's Ten Commandments. Traditionally thought of only as a guide to living a good life and as a way of preparing themselves to enter heaven, the Ten Commandments are actually a set of instructions for saving the energy needed to experience "God" and to have a personal relationship with "God".

Chance encounters with what we have called "God" have inspired people to create churches and societies dedicated to worshiping this inspiration. But it has also motivated the misguided to suppress and eliminate those who deny its existence or worship it in a different way. When the perception of what we have called "God" occurs, the type and quality of that experience is filtered through the expectations and predilections of the one experiencing it, leading to the multitude of ways that "God" is worshiped.

Unfortunately, those who actually see "God" usually have only enough energy to have this experience one time. "God" is experienced as the sum total of all the good things about mankind. Kindness, generosity, reverence, beauty and many other attributes of humanity seem to be contained in the vision before us. It always overwhelms the person experiencing it for the first and (usually) only time. A warrior, on the other hand, has the extreme energy to place her assemblage point precisely at that spot on her luminous energy shell to experience "God" when she so desires. And this experience has shown warriors that what we have called "God" is a static vision that has no power to alter, affect or change anything. It is in fact a celebration of all that is good about mankind, but since patting ourselves on the back is self-important behavior, "God" is a reflection of our own self-importance.

What we call science is also merely a reflection of ourselves, of the modality of the times we live in. And since predatory self-importance rules our way of thinking, it must also rule science. Objectivity is determined by the prevailing wisdom and beliefs of the time period in which it is pursued. And since objectivity is the basis of all science, it will reflect only those attitudes. As long as our attitudes and beliefs are ruled exclusively by self-importance, the predator's mind, science will be also.

The intellectual self-absorption of science separates us from the world and from our own true nature. We become strangers to ourselves and strangers in a strange world that will not conform to our self-important intellectual expectations. Neither our bodies nor our consciousness can be defined by the expectations of science. We are supposed to be like a chunk of metal that can be pounded into any shape desired. But we are not solid. We are not objects. We are too elusive and ethereal for such a simplistic explanation. To reduce an unfathomable mystery to a mathematical equation is moronic and disrespectful to the value and complexity of human life. Human life has no more value to the scientist than the life of a microbe grown in a Petri dish. As our infatuation with science grows we will be treated more and more as an abstract, disposable commodity, as Joseph Stalin regarded the people of the Soviet Union during his reign of terror. When science takes total control, unimaginable horror is soon to follow.

Those who pride themselves on being rational and objective are also very often those who immerse themselves in the irrationality of alcohol, drugs, sex, art and music. Art and music are often considered to be the products of the highly organized and rational portion of the mind, but since they are designed to alter the perception of the beholder they belong more properly in the realm of the irrational. The rational immerse themselves in the irrational as an escape, a respite from the pressure and stress of their lives. Does anyone see a contradiction here?

Another glaring contradiction is the attribution of scientific breakthroughs to "creativity." Creativity is an intuitive, non-linear and irrational process that makes connections which are at first seemingly illogical. Only after "creativity" occurs do scientists construct what they call logical explanations. In other words, the rational is built on the irrational. The rational built on the irrational?

Scratch the surface of any rational person and one finds the mystic waiting to emerge. Since the possibility of expanding our perception is our birthright and natural state, ruling out the possibility of perceiving the world in any but one way is deleterious and very often results in self-destructive behaviors. We unconsciously sense the necessity of exploring our mystical side and very often end up destroying ourselves in that pursuit.

7. The 1960's

In the 1960's, the desire to explore our mystical and spiritual side changed from being the concern of only a small minority to one that affected millions. The affluence generated during the 1950's enabled a lifestyle for many that gave them the time to reflect on the emptiness of materialism and the seeming impotence of established religious and philosophical systems in addressing this condition. People looked around and saw the nearly universal conformity that suppressed individual expression and creativity. A look at any high school or college yearbook from this era reveals the uniformity of dress and hairstyles that reflected this relentless conformity. Youth in particular saw that their parents' quest for material acquisition blinded them to the importance of having meaningful relationships with each other, their children and their parents. It became obvious that the widespread abuse of alcohol and prescription drugs was the method by which society was insulating itself from the reality of spiritual emptiness. The result was a massive rejection, especially by youth, of the "values" and totems that had led to what many felt to be the spiritual and philosophical stagnation of Western culture.

What I consider to be a major tipping point in this transition was the Cuban Missile crisis of October 1962. Millions of people in the West were suddenly confronted with the possibility of sudden and violent death at the push of a button. Another tipping point was the assassination of President Kennedy in November of 1963. If even the President of the United States could be cut down by an assassin(s)' violence, how safe was anyone else? And how should we live our lives in the face of the possibility of sudden death? Should we continue to live within the customs and mores which created an increasingly violent world or look for alternatives?

So, the search began. It was not enough to question only the violent and materialistic lifestyle practiced by Western culture, but also the mindset that led to the unthinking acceptance of this lifestyle. How to alter that mindset led to an exploration of the use of psychoactive drugs, particularly marijuana and LSD, that, it was hoped, would alter the thought patterns that had led the West into a materialistic wasteland, a spiritual desert. Alternative forms of spirituality from other cultures became an important source of inspiration for those seeking an effective and fulfilling spiritual life. Prevailing attitudes toward sexual expression were questioned and then rejected.

But, as time passed, it became increasingly obvious that the chaotic experimentation of the 1960's was not leading to a new order, a more fulfilling life, but only more chaos. Positive energy that had embarked on a new course - a noble endeavor - was dissipated rapidly in a whirlpool of drug abuse and sexual obsession. This energetic dissipation led straight back to the same sense of emptiness and enervation that had prompted the rejection of the customs of the 1950's. Now all roads led to the same end, and the disillusionment that this result prompted has informed Western culture ever since, fragmenting it into many mini-cultures that often overlap in their customs and mores, but are essentially equal in their spiritual and philosophical aridity.

8. The Authenticity of Castaneda's Reportage

The copyright of Castaneda's first book, *The Teachings of Don Juan*, belonged to the University of California at Los Angeles (UCLA) where Castaneda was completing his graduate work in anthropology. To suggest that UCLA's Dept. of Anthropology would allow their academic reputation to be attached to fiction masquerading as fact is absurd. Merely because Castaneda wrote that don Juan refused to fill out forms or allow photographs or sound recordings doesn't mean that none were ever made or that UCLA's Department of Anthropology never confirmed don Juan's existence. They would not have allowed the publication of the book under their aegis without such confirmation. The fact that they respected don Juan's right to privacy by not discussing the means of confirmation cannot be taken to mean that such confirmation never occurred.

Don Juan was sophisticated enough to know that UCLA would never allow the publication of *The Teachings of Don Juan* without objective confirmation. Since it was don Juan's task to explain the Warrior's Way to the outside world, he would have taken whatever steps were necessary. At least one sound recording of don Juan's voice may exist. Castaneda's second book, *A Separate Reality (Further Conversations with Don Juan),* states that don Juan was present at a small gathering Castaneda attended with don Juan's grandson Lucio and several other men in September of 1968 and that Castaneda was documenting this meeting with a tape recorder. Castaneda did not reveal if don Juan's voice was actually recorded on this tape, but the incident clearly indicates that at least one recording may exist and that don Juan was not actually averse to the possibility of having his voice recorded.

Those who refer to Castaneda's books as brilliant works of fiction ignore the incredibly banal existence that Castaneda lived apart from don Juan and that the true power and beauty of the books comes exclusively from don Juan's own words, which could have been transcribed by anyone fluent in both Spanish and English. No one as brilliant as some claim

Castaneda was could possibly have led such an idiotic life as a tyrannical, sexually obsessed control freak. Don Juan was quite serious when he introduced Castaneda to his cohorts Vicente Medrano and Silvio Manuel as "by far the biggest indulger that I've ever met." And he was certainly too stupid to have constructed the Warrior's Way out of his own imagination or even from gleanings from the work of others. Giving Castaneda credit for the Warrior's Way is like giving Walter Cronkite credit for men walking on the moon. Castaneda was a participant/reporter, not an originator.

The big problem that Western academia/journalism has with the Warrior's Way is that it puts their "knowledge" quite in the shade. It makes their "knowledge" irrelevant, outdated and primitive. The Warrior's Way threatens the established social and economic orders of all societies. And that is why that don Juan has to remain a myth, a fiction. The alternative is unthinkable for those so heavily invested, psychologically and financially, in the present social order. And for a system of knowledge as powerful and engulfing as the Warrior's Way to have been promulgated by a mere Indian such as don Juan is totally unacceptable to the legions of academics who assume that anyone who would dare to comment upon the basic nature of reality must have a PhD certificate hanging on the wall of their office. A similar cultural chauvinism has been visited upon Castaneda also. That a simple student of anthropology would be chosen to disseminate the Warrior's Way, and not one of the academic elite, is equally unacceptable.

The opposition to the emergence of the Warrior's Way will be vicious and violent. Those who advocate it will be attacked in any possible way that the detractors can find. A good example of this can be found in the writings of Richard de Mille (See Appendix V). His books are cited as an expose that debunks the Warrior's Way by those who have obviously never read them (either de Mille's or all of Castaneda's). De Mille's first book was so obviously filled with envy, jealousy and sarcasm that it was instantly rejected by the academics that de Mille wished to impress and convince, forcing him to write a second one. But it was no better, its one distinctive feature, a section called the Alleglossary, being the only part used by skeptics to attack Castaneda's reportage. Even the author's portrait in the second book was used to express de Mille's dismally sarcastic attitude. As for the Alleglossary, de Mille merely assigned ownership of every idiom in the English language to an author whose work was published before Castaneda's books, and some to authors whose work was published after Castaneda's. But de Mille's curious silence after the publication of his second book is telling. He could obviously find no even remotely related precedent or forerunner to the totally unique concepts that Castaneda reported in his books from *The Eagle's Gift* forward.

One advantage that critics like de Mille have had in attacking Castaneda's early books is that Castaneda himself was confused about the ultimate goal (reaching the Third Attention) of the Warrior's Way and the precise technique (manipulation of the position of the assemblage point) used to reach that goal. It was only in the books from *The Eagle's Gift* forward that Castaneda began to get a handle on the Warrior's Way and report it a much more accurate and articulate manner. And since Castaneda's death critics and journalists have become obsessed with the details of his sordid lifestyle, which enables them to brush the Warrior's Way aside and indulge in sensationalist rhetoric like barkers on a circus midway.

The power and truth of the words of don Juan endure untouched, unaffected. And will always remain so.

9. The Transition to the Third Attention

"...warriors can never make a bridge to join the people of the world. But, if people desire to do so, they have to make a bridge to join warriors." (8,5,213)

Warriors refer to our awareness in this world as the First Attention. The ability to perceive other worlds, other universes real or imaginary, is called the Second Attention. But the achievement of the ultimate perceptual possibility available to us is referred to as the Third Attention.

The mechanism by which a warrior enters the Third Attention was described by don Juan in several ways; the most basic description is that the energy inside the luminous shell is made to merge with the energy outside of it, becoming an active part of that energy while still maintaining the individual's awareness.

A more detailed explanation begins with the fact that our luminous energy shell contains the same energetic emanations as lie outside the luminous shell. But the assemblage point only lights up—makes available to our perception—a very small number of these emanations at any one time. By intending the assemblage point to move instantly across the entire luminous shell, all the energetic emanations inside the shell light up—are made available to our perception—at once. This breaks the boundaries of the luminous shell and the emanations within fuse with those without, maintaining the individual's awareness while becoming part of the all-encompassing outside awareness. The energy and awareness that had been separated from its source by the boundaries of the luminous energy shell returns to that source and becomes an active part of the infinite.

It should be made clear that the transition to the Third Attention leaves behind no residue, no corpse. Our entire bodily awareness is instantly transformed into pure energy, pure awareness; a specialized, hi-speed, independent inorganic being capable of sustaining itself by tapping directly into the Earth's energy. One can no longer experience the sensual pleasures of our present mode of existence, but one can still observe life in this world. We just can't actively participate in it with our full bodily awareness.

However, there is a brief, rather mysterious reference in *The Second Ring Of Power* to the possibility that those in the Third Attention can return to this world, but in the form of a very tiny creature such as a small insect. It is not known whether this is done on a temporary, intermittent or permanent basis or what level of awareness or activity is possible by one who does it. Castaneda and the other apprentices that Don Juan had gathered for what was to be Castaneda's warrior party were extremely confused about how to proceed on the warrior's path at this point, so it is impossible to say what significance that this reference has.

We do know that one who has reached the Third Attention can project his image back into this world in much the same way that a movie projector projects light onto a movie screen. We know this because that don Juan is known to have done so twice. The first incidence was reported in *The Eagle's Gift*, when don Juan and don Genaro were spotted by Castaneda and Maria Elena (La Gorda) in Oaxaca. They were not able to speak to them or interact with them but Maria Elena believed that don Juan and don Genaro were trying to give them a subtle message about what steps they should take next to move forward on the warrior's path. The second incident, reported by Castaneda's on-again-off-again companion Amy Wallace in her book *Sorcerer's Apprentice*, was in San Francisco, where don Juan was seen by Florinda Donner-Grau (one of the two apprentices of Castaneda's second warrior's party) and Carol Tiggs (the nagual woman).

What is doubly intriguing about the first incident is that at one point, don Genaro beckoned Castaneda and Maria Elena with a movement of his head. Castaneda was the only one who saw don Genaro do this and when he later mentioned it to the other apprentices they informed him that don Genaro had told them that when it was time for them to leave the valley where they lived he would somehow let them know with a movement of his head. Don Genaro had planned in advance to communicate with them from the Third Attention.

We also know that those who have reached the Third Attention may be able to communicate directly with those in this world through dreaming. In *The Eagle's Gift*, both Josefina and Maria Elena stated that they had communicated with Eligio, don Juan's most talented apprentice. Eligio's predilection for the warrior's world was so extreme that he joined don Juan's party in their move to the Third Attention. Why that Eligio chose to reach out to the fellow apprentices that he left behind is, of course, unknown. But he did give both Josefina and Maria Elena vital information about the relationship of Castaneda to don Juan and don Genaro's other apprentices.

But if it is possible for those in the Third Attention to meet in dreaming with warriors still in this world, it could be a tremendous boost to those whose leadership will be responsible for the final act in human history this time around—the move to the Third Attention of millions and perhaps billions of people. It is certainly an exciting and intriguing possibility ripe for discussion and research. Perhaps we merely have to intend it until our command becomes the spirit's command. Only time will tell.

10. Psychoactive Plants and the Warrior's Way

Don Juan administered psychoactive plant preparations to some of his apprentices (such as Castaneda) who were "empty", those had parented children. Becoming a parent saps the energy of the parent and leaves a hole in the luminous energy shell. A parent's assemblage point is locked down in its usual position even tighter than that of a non-parent's is because a parent lacks the energy needed to move it away from its customary position. For non-parents, those who are still "complete," the traditional methods of moving the assemblage point (stopping the internal dialogue, controlling dreams, stalking oneself, etc.) are more than adequate for setting this process in motion.

These plant preparations were prepared and administered to apprentices under very tightly controlled conditions only. These techniques are in a very different universe from the often random and chaotic conditions that those who have taken psychoactive drugs in an attempt to "expand their consciousness" have subjected themselves to. The experiences resulting from this sort of carelessness were all too often horror and madness.

But the people of don Juan's time on Earth were very different from those alive today. Many, if not most of them, grew up in very stable conditions. This resulted in their assemblage points being locked down very tightly. Such is not the case today. The relentless bombardment of horrific and disturbing images from the media, the prevalence of divorce, and the wide assortment of psychoactive drugs available (including mood-altering prescriptions widely administered by doctors) have all resulted in a very different person. The lack of stability and sense of safety that modern people have experienced has resulted in a much less stable assemblage point. So at this point in our collective experience, I believe that psychoactive drug use to loosen the position of the assemblage point of "empty" people may be no longer necessary. And it is certainly never necessary for those who are still "complete."

Drug and alcohol use by those who have begun the process of moving their assemblage points by using the techniques described in the Warrior's Way is very dangerous and could prove fatal. One's awareness could enter unknown realms of the Second Attention and never return. Worlds as real and predatory as this one is could be reached by accident and result in a warrior's very real death in those worlds. Another very real possibility is that a warrior could become the prisoner of beings who immobilize the position of a warrior's assemblage point, making the perception of that world the only possible one. That condition is analogous to humanity's present predicament. Our parents and teachers have taught us to immobilize our assemblage points in the one position that allows only the perception of the world of everyday life.

A warrior strives to always remain in total control of the position and movement of the assemblage point. She would never take a chance of losing the control that she has worked so hard to create and maintain. Such random shifts of the assemblage point as those induced by drugs are the very opposite of the discipline that warriors strive to maintain.

No drug-induced experience could ever match the exhilaration and pure joy that a warrior experiences when he first begins to take control of his *dreaming* and begins to have some success in practicing the other methods of moving the assemblage point. Perceptual possibilities far more breathtaking than any drug experience could provide await those warriors with the discipline to follow the warrior's path in a sober, detached and disciplined way.

Human will is more powerful than any drug or psychoactive plant preparation could ever be, or ever will be.

" ...freedom cannot be an investment. Freedom is an adventure with no end, in which we risk our lives and much more for a few moments of something beyond words, beyond thoughts or feelings. To seek freedom is the only driving force I know. Freedom to fly off into that infinity out there. Freedom to dissolve; to lift off; to be like the flame of a candle, which, in spite of being up against the light of a billion stars, remains intact, because it never pretended to be more than what it is, a mere candle." (9,4,81)

11. Energy, Creativity and Wellness

Artists are those whose assemblage point moves freely. Due to childhood experiences and/or trauma, their assemblage point never acquired the stability that others have. The free movement of the assemblage point sparks creativity and imagination, almost enabling the artist to live in the worlds that they are imagining.

So, of what use is this information? The practical value is immense both for artists and for those who seek creative solutions to day-to-day problems. Now an artist seeking inspiration can move her assemblage point instead of the usual maneuvers that artists often indulge themselves in such as drinking, using drugs, sex, rage or merely waiting for inspiration to show up. The energy saved by avoiding these activities can be applied to the creation of their art, giving the work of an artist/warrior a power unknown to those who spend more time in dissipation than creation. Those who have energy create. Those without do not.

Artists should also be aware of the effect of their association with strong personalities. These folks have very rigid assemblage points but are very energetic and can cause an artist's assemblage point to stabilize. This brings temporary relief from the incessant movement of the assemblage point that the artist is used to and can be very comforting, but can also stop the movement of the assemblage point that leads to creativity in the first place.

Maximum energy equals maximum creativity. Maximum energy means the power to have a vision and to bring it to life. So anything that reduces energy reduces creativity. The movement of an creative person's assemblage point to a new set of feelings, a different take on reality, provides the moment of inspiration. Without the energy to move the assemblage point, real inspiration is not possible. Artists/writers/creators have often used various experiences (very often sex) and substances (alcohol and drugs) to move their assemblage points with inevitably deteriorating results. The result of these techniques reduces the creative person's overall energy level and real creativity disappears. How fast it goes is determined by the amount of energy each person has to start with and how fast that their individual store of energy is used up.

The Warrior's Way has also provided a very interesting take on the creative process - the idea that one cannot make the same choice over and over immediately. The creative mind is like a gun that can only fire once and must be reloaded, a process that takes a certain amount of time. A fine example of this was related by the author Hunter Davies in his authorized biography of The Beatles. He was allowed to sit in on songwriting sessions with two of the most creatively gifted people of the 20th century, John Lennon and Paul McCartney. His take on the situation was that they often seemed to be only goofing around with very little serious work being done. But in actuality they were taking the time to reload the creative gun, so to speak, before making their next compositional choice.

It is well known that many creative people work almost exclusively during the late night/early morning hours of the day. I believe that this is an unconscious response to what warriors call the fixation of the first attention of other people. While awake, others can subtly interfere with the energy field of whoever they concentrate their attention on. Human will can extend itself over great distances in ways that can influence our energy field in positive or negative ways. One illustration of this phenomenon is shown in studies which demonstrate that sick patients who are prayed for by others recover better than those who are not prayed for. Those praying are actually affecting the energy field of those being prayed for by placing their attention on them, even from far away. Conversely, focusing negative attention can have subtly adverse effects on us as well.

Maximum energy means maximum wellness, both physically and psychologically. Maximum energy means maximum resistance of the body to disease. Young people, with their strong energy are seldom subject to serious illness. But as we age, our energy level declines and the body's resistance begins to break down. The rapidity of this decline is determined by the amount of energy the body has at the start and the toll that our lifestyle choices and experiences take on us as we age. The techniques that the Warrior's Way offers for conserving energy (conserving sexual energy, dropping self-importance, recapitulation) can guarantee a healthy existence for many years after the body should theoretically have begun to break down.

Taken from don Juan's insistence that drinking alcohol and caffeinated beverages uses up too much energy and damages the body, I have personally extrapolated a belief that only natural food and drink can be assimilated by the body without causing damage/energy loss. Avoiding man-made substances avoids unnecessary damage.

Don Juan stated that a person's psychological health is determined by the variety and fluidity of their internal dialogue. A repetitive internal dialogue results in boredom, depression and madness. But to vary the internal dialogue requires energy. Conserving energy gives us that ability, to pull ourselves out of the well of negativity (or overconfidence) that can drown us. The ability to curtail our self-importance, to laugh at ourselves, is particularly important in this area. One trick that don Juan suggested to Castaneda was to tell himself the opposite of what his negative thoughts were repeatedly telling him. And then to realize that both are equally unreal, unnecessary and self-important. The technique of recapitulation can also relieve the psychological pressure of past experiences, resulting in a more positive internal dialogue.

One of the reasons that warriors avoid confronting others bluntly is to avoid the energy loss that results from these high-tension situations and the self-important feelings of guilt and self-recrimination that often occur afterwards. One loses energy in the confrontation and then dissipates even more in the storm of negative internal dialogue that follows. Don Juan stated a hard truth : no one is doing anything to anyone. How we react to the actions of our fellow men is entirely our choice. We can detach ourselves from deleterious self-concern or fall victim to it. It is our choice.

"A warrior makes his own mood. You didn't know that. Fear

[Don Juan and Castaneda were chased by a jaguar] got you into the mood of a warrior, but now that you know about it, anything can serve to get you into it. It's convenient to always act in such a mood. It cuts through the crap and leaves one purified. One needs the mood of a warrior for every single act. Otherwise one becomes distorted and ugly. There is no power in a life that lacks this mood. Look at yourself. Everything offends and upsets you. A warrior, on the other hand ... calculates everything. That's control. But once his calculations are over, he acts. He lets go. That's abandon. For a warrior there is nothing offensive about the acts of his fellow men as long as he himself is acting within the proper mood. The other night you were not offended by the jaguar. The fact that it chased us did not anger you. I did not hear you cursing it, nor did I hear you say that he had no right to follow us. To achieve the mood of a warrior is not a simple matter. It is a revolution. To regard the jaguar...and our fellow men as equals is a magnificent act of the warrior's spirit. It takes power to do that." (3,11,149-151)

12. The Conditions of Modern Life

We intuitively sense that there is much more to ourselves than the rational mind can comprehend. But the gospel of objectivity, of science, gives us no words to express these feelings. That's because the knowledge, the wisdom we seek has no words. It is pure action. As our internal dialogue goes round and round trying to express the inexpressible, we become exhausted and frustrated. So we substitute our mundane internal dialogue with that of others through television, movies, books, music, etc. But since these new words are the products of those whose internal dialogue is just as mundane–and almost exclusively the product of the rational mind –they are no help.

Action takes energy, and we have very little. Very few people in the modern world have not dissipated their energy through greed, obesity, drugs, alcohol, sex or self-importance. If we are not passively submerged in various media, we engage in furious activity that leaves us drained. But these relentless, restless distractions are also meaningless. Again, there are no words for the meaning we seek, it can only be experienced. It requires action, but we have no energy for action. However, that can be changed. It requires discipline–the discipline to conserve our energy, stop our useless internal dialogue and let intent, the spirit, take over.

One begins with a single act that is sustained until it develops into what warriors call unbending intent. Our awareness gathers speed and strength like a snowball rolling down a snowy hill. The assemblage point begins to move from its usual position, revealing the breathtaking possibilities of our hidden resources, our untapped awareness.

It is actually a very simple process. But having the energy to start and maintain that process in a modern world of scientific cynicism is not simple at all. When we began to trust exclusively the concatenations of the rational mind we lost something that we intuitively know to be irreplaceable–our true nature as a mysterious part of an awesome and unfathomable universe. The higher men build their facade of reason, the farther it has to fall.

Our minds become so overcrowded with millions of contradictory "facts" and suppositions that we turn into punch-drunk boxers; thinking we can punch our way through a maze of contradictions to a synthesis that satisfies our reason when in reality it takes only a glancing blow from the unknown to bring us to our knees. Very few of us have the insight to realize that no matter how much we think we know, there an infinitely greater amount that we don't know. Fewer still have the humility to accept that there is so much more we can never know and can never even hope to comprehend.

Even as Western societies slide deeper into decadence, dissipation and chaos, I remain optimistic. I know that almost everyone seeks a way out of this madness that seems inescapable. People crave discipline and integrity and the Warrior's Way offers these in abundance. I know that as more and more of us conserve our energy and open ourselves to the intent of the Spirit our personal power will increase exponentially. This will attract many others to follow our example until the future of the human race is re-imagined and remade.

There is no stopping the Warrior's Way. It is as inevitable as the sunrise. The only question is how long that the change will take. There is no power on Earth that has the energy or the will to stop us. We are the future, and the future is now. We are not saying that anyone else is wrong or that we are right. There is no debate. We will lead by example.

13. The Misunderstanding

If one reads only the first few Castaneda books it would be easy to get the impression that the objective of the Warrior's Way is about the acquisition of "power." And how that "power" was to be used was left undefined. This was caused by a combination of what Castaneda chose to emphasize and don Juan's teaching method. Castaneda was instructed in his normal awareness and also when don Juan moved Castaneda's assemblage point into what is called heightened awareness.

When Castaneda was in his normal awareness, don Juan tailored his instruction to Castaneda's character and personality; a character which, as later events showed, left much to be desired. Castaneda could most readily recall events that occurred in his normal awareness, when he was being catered to. Thus the emphasis on "power."

The more engulfing, abstract concepts of the Warrior's Way that might seem too startling for a warrior's normal awareness were given to Castaneda in heightened awareness, which impairs memory when normal awareness is returned to. A way of thinking about heightened awareness is to compare it to trying to remember a dream upon awakening. Sometimes one can only recall bits and pieces of some dreams and as we wake more completely even those pieces fade. To remember the dream completely the assemblage point has to move back to the position it was in while dreaming. The same difficulty applies to trying to remember concepts and instructions received while in heightened awareness. Castaneda could remember very little of the instruction that he had received in heightened awareness until after don Juan and his party left the world. His interactions with Maria Elena and the other apprentices in that period triggered the recollection process. Meeting Maria Elena again, in particular, was like meeting a character from a dream. Meeting someone from a dream (or dreams) in real life would undoubtedly inspire an intense recollection of the dream(s) in question.

This process of remembering the instruction received while in heightened awareness is prescribed in The Rule Of The

Nagual. After the nagual and his party leave the world, the nagual's apprentices are "commanded to forget" and must begin recalling and reorganizing the training received in their normal awareness and in heightened awareness.

An understanding of this procedure is crucial for anyone reading Castaneda's books. The first five books were almost exclusively information Castaneda could remember from his normal awareness. The last seven books were an integration of the training he received in both states of awareness.

It was an apprentice' long term goal to save enough energy to return the assemblage point to the position that enables the recall of instruction given while in heightened awareness. Castaneda managed to remember much of what he was taught in heightened awareness before his lifestyle depleted his energy and killed him, but we will never know exactly how much was lost.

14. The Flyers

The flyers (or "mud shadows") have become a topic of intense interest and near obsession for some of those who have read *The Active Side of Infinity*. The flyers were described by don Juan as an alien intelligence that feeds on the energy shell of humans and has a certain amount of control over our internal dialogue. One phenomenon that suggests we are not totally in control of our thought process, our internal dialogue, is what happens to the internal dialogue as we fall asleep. What had been a coherent stream of thought spirals into a nonsensical mishmash of disconnected ideas and images as sleep approaches. This would seem to contradict the idea that thoughts must be formed and intended before they cross our minds; that we are in control of them. How can we truly be in control if the internal dialogue continues to spout unintended nonsense until the instant we fall asleep? And if we are not in control then who, or what is?

Don Juan said that we have two minds. The dominant mind is what he called a "foreign installation" given to us by the flyers. Our true mind is relegated to the far background, but still remains. The flyers mind is the insecure, shifty, conflicted predator's mind. Our true mind is what gives hope, peace, and purpose. A warrior's discipline—summoned by his unbending intent to follow the Warrior's Way—makes the predator's mind flee, leaving behind only the true mind. Because we have been conditioned to act only through the predator's mind, when it flees we are left with the mind we have never really used before and must learn to use instead. At this point it becomes more important than ever to live like a warrior, as that is the only guideline we have left.

Because the discipline of living like a warrior makes them irrelevant, the flyers are of no long term importance—a curiosity.

However, discipline requires action. The Warrior's Way is a prescription for action, not an abstract philosophical thesis. The Warrior's Way was traditionally taught by word of mouth in a natural setting where the particular technique being imparted was immediately put into practice in the real world. As Castaneda's apprenticeship details, it was often sink or swim. That is a far different reality than sitting in a comfortable chair and reading the books like philosophical texts requiring thought alone.

Having a teacher—a nagual to guide them—would seem to give warriors trained in the traditional manner a big advantage. However, as don Juan stated, the only real advantage of having a teacher is to have someone to spur a warrior to action. And he also stated that impeccable men and women need no one to guide them. In reality the nagual/apprentice relationship was cumbersome and required many years of often fruitless talk and activity in order to even begin to approach the most important technique of all, moving the assemblage point. Modern warriors start from a vantage point that makes the objectives of the Warrior's Way clear from the beginning. As is evident in his books, Castaneda spent his entire apprenticeship in a state of utter confusion. A modern warrior can avoid such confusion because she has the record of Castaneda's experience and the complete statements of Don Juan from which to begin her journey to the spirit.

A warrior proceeds on the practical and abstract levels simultaneously. On the practical level he is learning to move his assemblage point but as this work continues he realizes that he is also seeking to become one with the spirit. A warrior acts only for the spirit. There is no other way. The self-importance of would-be warriors acting only for themselves will destroy them. There is no progress on the Warrior's Path without the intervention of the spirit. Any warrior who believes that he is doing it all himself is bound to fail. Fates worse than death await the warrior who succumbs to self-importance. Warriors know that death is the end of perception. But a careless, self-important warrior can become the prisoner of other awareness from distant realms and this imprisonment and slavery can extend into eons, a truly horrible fate.

Temptations of power and indulgence are always fatal for a warrior, as they were for Castaneda.

15. The Sexual Obsession

"I have always told you that sexual energy is something of ultimate importance and that it has to be controlled and used with great care. But you have always resented what I said, because you thought I was speaking of control in terms of morality; I always meant it in terms of saving and rechanneling energy." (7,4,69)

Western society has turned sex into a freak show, a commodity. People speak of having sex with the same passion with which they would order a cup of coffee. Sex is for making babies, to create and perpetuate awareness. Sexual behavior has traditionally been among the most tightly controlled and regulated aspects of any human behavior in all societies. This control has usually been considered to be a result of religious or societal standards of morality, but is actually the result of the unspoken, sometimes unconscious, knowledge that sex dissipates intellectual, physical and spiritual energy faster than any other activity. The cultures that have practiced the most repressive control of sexuality have turned out to be those that have dominated all the others, for better or ill. Nothing beats sexual energy. Societies that conserve it thrive and dominate. Those that dissipate it weaken and fall.

However, people have the power of choice. If they choose to be disease-prone and weakened physically, spiritually and psychologically, good luck to them. They won't have any, though. You make your own luck by having and saving energy. Good things happen to those with energy. Bad things happen to those without. The spirit enters each life regardless. It transforms those with energy and destroys those without it.

"[Warriors] know that the only real energy we possess is a life-bestowing sexual energy. This knowledge makes them permanently conscious of their responsibility." (7,4,71)

It is not surprising that sex has become an obsession. As one of the few things (and it's pathetic to be able to describe a human relationship as a "thing," but that is how sex is now regarded) that provide any sort of excitement or novelty to those not totally jaded or dissipated, it is an endless topic for gossip and discussion. In a bored and decadent culture, what else is there? Progress in the arts and sciences has ground to a halt, or a glacial crawl. Sports are merely a repetitive form of theatre. Politics has become only another sport, with the media showing no interest in the ideas, only the horse race. The latest technological advances seem designed only for the more efficient gathering and storage of information. "New" art, books, movies, theatre, music and dance are invariably a variation or restatement of what has come before. They have nothing new to say so they end up going in circles like a cat chasing its own tail.

There are new things to say, but that would require a fundamental reappraisal of our way of perceiving life and the world. It would require a level of discomfort that modern culture finds anathema. We seem to have temporarily subdued the natural world in order to provide adequately for our material well-being. The fact that it has left us spiritually empty is an inevitable by-product, but largely viewed as a self-indulgent aberration or inconvenience. "Stop complaining. You never had it so good"–this seems to be the dominant attitude towards those who seek a more meaningful and fulfilling spiritual life.

In the 1960's and afterward there has been a great deal of interest in alternatives to traditional Western spirituality, but these are almost always other traditional forms of spirituality from other cultures. And when they clash with, and are overridden by, modernity's sex-obsessed materialism, they provide no more solace than the old forms they replaced.

One interesting sidelight to traditional spirituality is the technique of intending in the second attention. A destination for perception is intended, created by practitioner(s) as an alternate place for perception to dwell. Considering that in some of the other worlds available to our awareness of time is altered significantly, perhaps these intended destinations could also share that altered sense of time. Since millions of people have focused their awareness on shared concepts (heaven, hell, nirvana, purgatory, etc.) to me it seems possible that their combined power of awareness has perhaps intended the creation of these as alternate, temporary destinations for perception. Those who are, because of illness, unconscious or in a comatose state, could possibly experience these temporary realities. If these realities also include an altered sense of time, it would theoretically be possible for a still-living awareness to remain in one of these places for what they perceive to be nearly an eternity. Since death is the end of perception, this possibility of perceiving intended realities ends also. Such a possibility might give pause to those who believe in nothing except themselves but have had concepts such as heaven and hell imprinted on their consciousness at a very early age.

"There is nothing wrong with man's sensuality. It's man's ignorance of and disregard for his magical nature that is wrong. (7,4,72)

16. Evil

"Of course, there is a dark side to us. We kill wantonly, don't we? We burn people in the name of God. We destroy ourselves; we obliterate life on this planet; we destroy the earth. And then we dress in robes and the Lord speaks directly to us. And what does the Lord tell us? He says that we should be good boys or he is going to punish us. The Lord has been threatening us for centuries and it doesn't make any difference. Not because we are evil, but because we are dumb. Man has a dark side, yes, and it's called stupidity." (8,6,284)

Warriors don't accept evil as an outside force that controls or influences human behavior. Evil does not cause stupidity, cruelty, meanness, indulgence, etc. These are some of the most virulent forms of self-importance, which governs almost all human endeavor. The concept of evil is one that churches and society at large uses as an excuse to absolve those it wishes to forgive while it condemns those it chooses not to forgive. It's part of the "forgive anything" religious ethos that enables even the most base and disgusting behavior with the promise of forgiveness. "It wasn't really him that did those awful things. He had been taken over by evil, so it's not really his fault. He should be forgiven. And if evil takes control of him again, he should be forgiven again." And of course this ethos of forgiveness is most repeatedly and generously applied to the rich and powerful.

Money and position are equated with hard work, industriousness and diligence - which are virtuous. Riches and power are seen to be gifts from God given to those most deserving of such gifts. Poverty is seen as a sign of weakness, indulgence and sloth—which are not virtuous. It is this religious-based bias which decrees that a poor person will be sent to prison for stealing a loaf of bread, but that wealthier individuals and groups go free for stealing thousands or even millions of dollars.

In the transition to popular acceptance of the Warrior's Way there will undoubtedly be would-be warriors of low character who use the possibilities afforded by the warrior's path to exploit and abuse others for personal gain. One example of this would be an individual who has struck a bargain with the inorganic beings. These individuals would agree to become the servants to the inorganic beings in exchange for a much extended life span and earthly powers that could involve actions that would harm others. The detractors of the Warrior's Way will point to these aberrant individuals and use them as an excuse to condemn the Warrior's Way as evil (and there will be those who see any variance from their religious beliefs found in the warrior's path as evil also). But the self-indulgent idiots that use the Warrior's Way to abuse others are not warriors. They are merely criminals. In every group of people there are aberrant individuals who abuse others. And society has the right and obligation to protect the vulnerable from them. But a true warrior has no need or desires other than to become one with the Spirit and the exploitation of others has nothing whatsoever to do with that goal.

Society's transition to the Warrior's Way will be chaotic, but not as much as I once feared. The individuals who might use their expanded powers of perception to manipulate or harm others will usually be too cynical or myopic to accept or explore the Warrior' Way, limiting their impact.

Those who will blame the Warrior's Way for the actions of a few rogue individuals will be those most invested materially and psychologically in the dog-eat-dog philosophy that is the present curse of the human race. They will feel that their wealth and prominence (and their ability to exploit others) will be jeopardized with the rise of the Warrior's Way. And they will be correct in this assumption. Gold, silver, platinum, diamonds and pearls have little value if no one wants them. Power means nothing if no one believes in the institutions and/or belief systems that provide it.

So resistance to the Warrior's Way will be strong, violent and often overwhelming–but ultimately futile. Because the reason for the gift of life is the enhancement of consciousness and the warrior's path is the most efficient and fruitful way that the Spirit's goal of enhancing consciousness can be accomplished, the Warrior's Way is unstoppable. There will be many setbacks and much suffering inflicted by the detractors of the Warrior's Way but all must bow before the will of the spirit. There is no other way.

"Solace, haven, fear, all of them are moods that you have learned without ever questioning their value. As one can see, the black magicians have already engaged all your allegiance. Our fellow men are the black magicians. And since you are with them, you too are a black magician. Think for a moment. Can you deviate from the path that they've lined up for you? No. Your thoughts and your actions are fixed forever in their terms. That is slavery. I, on the other hand, brought you freedom. Freedom is expensive, but the price is not impossible. So, fear your captors, your masters. Don't waste your time and power fearing me." (4,1,28-29)

17. The Beginnings of the Warrior's Way

Modern warriors are the energetic descendants of the ancient Toltecs, a civilization which existed in central and southern Mexico thousands of years before the arrival of the Spanish. Don Juan said that they started on the path to knowledge by, accidentally or purposefully, consuming psychoactive plants indigenous to that region. Over many generations they became more and more aware of the possibilities for expanded awareness and personal power that were the result of the movement of the assemblage point caused by the ingestion of what they called power plants. Among these were peyote, Jimson weed and hallucinogenic mushrooms. With the passage of time they learned how to precisely prepare and use these plants to produce altered states of consciousness. As with any group of people engaged in exploring the nature of life and awareness, a gradual split developed among them as to which aspects of their knowledge should be emphasized and pursued.

The old seers, the warriors of the Second Attention as don Juan termed them, were interested in using their knowledge to accumulate power over their fellow men; often in deleterious and violent ways. They discovered the existence of inorganic beings and developed elaborate rituals and procedures for coming into contact with them and using them for their personal gain, or so they believed. They became so enamored of their inorganic allies that they sought to emulate them and achieve the same extremely long life span of the inorganic beings by living with them in the inorganic beings' world. But by doing so they placed their lives and energy in the service of the inorganic beings; becoming their servants, their slaves. Visiting the realm of the inorganic beings gave them a tremendous energy boost, a boost that don Juan maintained was necessary for any warrior who wishes to perfect the art of dreaming. But they made the mistake of believing they controlled that which actually enslaved them by catering to their most base and self-important desires.

But the new seers, the warriors of the Third Attention, were appalled and disgusted by the practices of the old seers that harmed their fellow men and ended with the old seers' enslavement by the inorganic beings. The warriors of the Third Attention were, and are, the seekers of total freedom. They wished to use the advances in knowledge gained by the old seers to increase their personal power in order to reach the Third Attention. To do this they developed a system of impeccable behavior, the Warrior's Way, that would lead to the goal of acquiescing to the designs of the abstract, the spirit. They found that this was the only reliable path to the achievement of their goal of freedom. Their commands became the spirit's commands, but only in the pursuit of forging a stronger connecting link to the spirit.

"The art of warriors is not really to choose, but to be subtle enough to acquiesce." (10,Introduction,7)

In time the new seers overcame the old seers and abolished the sorcery practices that they found so unnatural and dangerous. But the old seers left behind many artifacts, burial grounds, statues and pyramids that were imbued with their power and influence. These sites and artifacts, to this day, are very dangerous for those pursuing the Warrior's Way and also for anyone unfortunate enough to come in contact with them. They are designed to move the assemblage point of the beholder to relive ancient events and rituals that could have a bad influence or even scare them to death. The burial grounds of the old seers are the most dangerous to anyone who comes across them. The old seers' bodies were buried in these places but they are not dead, far from it. They live in these places with their inorganic masters and await those who stumble upon them so that they can feast on their energy as they scare them to death.
Certain geographical areas are also known to foster movements of the assemblage point that result in belligerent and warlike attitudes. The Sonoran desert is known to be one such area. Its effect on the assemblage point is also known to be efficacious for aberrant seers who wish to adopt animal

forms. The knowledge that entire regions can influence the movements of the assemblage points of their inhabitants seems particularly applicable when one considers the history of the Middle East. Conflict, hatred and war have been endemic to this region for centuries, as well as the founding of two of the world's major religions. This leads me to believe that this area is one that influences the movement of the assemblage point in extreme ways.

18. Inorganic Beings

Inorganic beings are one of the strangest phenomena presented to us by the Warrior's Way. A sentient living being that has no solid form is far outside the traditional view of consensual reality. We are familiar with the concept of ghosts or spirits that occasionally make their presence known among us, but they are not usually regarded as being real in the same sense that we regard ourselves as real. And they most certainly don't inhabit a world of their own where they exist independently in large numbers.

In all likelihood the vast majority of spirits and apparitions that can't be traced to the deaths of people are inorganic beings that have escaped or been drawn out of their realm by those who have contacted them intentionally or inadvertently. For example, after don Juan and don Genaro left this world for the Third Attention, their allies—the inorganic beings that were their helpers—were left to roam aimlessly in the general vicinity of don Juan and don Genaro's homes.

Because inorganic beings take on whatever form in this world that we project onto them, the wide variety of descriptions that have been given for strange apparitions and spirits will be as varied as the differences in the individuals who encounter them. But inorganic beings don't inhabit this world only in the guise of incomprehensible specters that go bump in the dark; they sometimes move among us disguised as ordinary people that seem to be going about their business like anyone else.

Don Juan accounted for the existence of inorganic beings when he stated that the Eagle's emanations that generate awareness are subdivided among the emanations that produce organic awareness and those that produce inorganic awareness. Inorganic beings are encased emanations of awareness without a solid, organic form. When *seen* as pure energy they look like a sleeping bag with a small zipper in the center. The "zipper" is actually a very thin, small gap in the continuity of their energetic shape. The size and structure of this gap explains the extraordinarily long duration of each inorganic being's existence in the following way: Throughout the lives of all sentient beings they are subject to constant assault by what is known as the rolling force, or the tumbler. It hits all living things constantly in conjunction with its sister force known as the circular force. The circular force hits just before each strike of the rolling force and imbues every sentient being with continuity and wholeness. The tumbler, however, is a force of disintegration. As a living being ages and loses energy it becomes more vulnerable to the strikes of the rolling force and dies when the tumbler breaks open the gap in the center of the energy shape; then the encased Eagle's emanations that provide life and awareness flood out of the energetic shell.

The small size and the configuration of the gap on an inorganic being's energy shape makes it very difficult for the tumbler to crack open. By contrast, the gap on a human being's luminous shell is much larger and more vulnerable to strikes from the rolling force, making its life span much, much shorter. According to don Juan, when a person begins to feel that the rolling force is hitting harder than the circular force, the rolling force hits harder and harder until that person dies. In other words, when someone loses hope and purpose and feels that life is too hard, death is soon to follow.

The inorganic beings live in their own world, their own universe, that is reachable by human awareness only with their cooperation. It appears to the energy body of a *dreamer* as a huge dark brown mass that looks like a sponge with a rough and porous texture. It consists of innumerable inorganic beings that live pressed together as long hollow tubes. The old sorcerers named it "the labyrinth of penumbra." Perhaps it was given that name because its complexity could easily cause a seer to become lost and trapped in it. When human awareness enters this world with its full physicality, it looks like a deserted yellow plain with thick yellow, fog-like vapors everywhere. The inorganic beings roam that plain hunting for any awareness that may venture there.

There are two kinds of inorganic beings; those whose energy shells contain some emanations like our own and those who have no emanations similar to ours. Most are of the latter type. The ones that share similar emanations are the ones that can interact and form relationships with human awareness. They have a low inherent energy level and seek the high-energy aura of *dreamers* to energize themselves.

To establish contact they send their scouts into our dreams. When a warrior turns his ordinary dreams into *dreaming*, they become fewer in number but more noticeable. A *dreamer* must be the one to first initiate contact; but once that solicitation is accomplished, a most dangerous and seductive symbiosis occurs. In return for a *dreamer's* high energy the inorganic beings teach secrets of manipulating awareness that are as bizarre, or as straightforward, as the *dreamer's* own personality. They customize their instruction—and their traps—to cater to a *dreamer's* most secret weaknesses and obsessions. And what they have to offer is tempting indeed to those who desire quick and easy gains.

A *dreamer* who agrees to live with them in their world will have his awareness extended "for nearly an eternity" by being shown how to re-structure his energy shape to closely resemble theirs. He will be instructed in methods of manipulating the awareness of other people to gain power and control over them. He can be taught how to transform himself into any other living thing that he has the energy to recreate. He can change his appearance at will. He will be allowed to witness distant realms and meet awareness from worlds unknown to us that have become trapped in the inorganic being's world. Imagine being able to interact with beings from distant galaxies and alternate universes that ordinary men could never even conceive of.

But the price for these favors is enslavement! Warriors who agree to live with the inorganic beings give up their freedom for the remainder of their existence. They become the servants of the inorganic beings' wishes no matter what they might be. A slave of the inorganic beings gives up his chance to enter the Third Attention; gives up his chance to become an independent inorganic being not beholden to the inorganic beings' world for his awareness that will last as long as the earth itself does.

Those who enter the Third Attention become part of the Eagle's emanations of awareness and so can visit any realm or interact with any awareness that the Eagle's emanations animates.

Reaching the Third Attention is difficult. It is much easier to become the slave of the inorganic beings. But the oppression of perpetual enslavement would undoubtedly eventually make the slave wish that he had died in this world as a free man.

A *dreamer* who does not wish to live with the inorganic beings but who continues to deal with them intimately can become their prisoner or meet his death. Warriors who wish to use the energy of the inorganic beings' world incautiously can be transported to realms where the assemblage point is fixed to one position, making the perception of that world the only possible one. Or the inorganic beings can play on the quirks of *dreamer's* personality to lure them into a battle that discharges all of the *dreamer's* energy, resulting in death. This kind of trap almost led to Castaneda's death. He barely survived.

The universe of the inorganic beings is female, so they seek male awareness in terms of trying to persuade male *dreamers* to live with them or attempting to imprison them. There are two examples in *The Art of Dreaming* of the inorganic beings abducting females and taking them into their world in their full physicality, but they were both paired with males at the time of their abduction. Experienced female *dreamers* can move in and out of that world at will - they have a scout available to them at all times - but the inorganic beings covet male awareness exclusively. They already have female awareness in abundance, so male awareness is a novelty, a different kind of energy.

The only valid reason that a true warrior has for dealing with the inorganic beings is that visiting their world gives her a energy boost that makes the movement of the assemblage point much easier. If it wasn't for that advantage they would be of no use at all. The only reason that don Juan and don Genaro had allies was they were given to them by their benefactor, the nagual Julian, before he left the world. Better to have them under control than lurking around menacingly, as they did to the apprentices after don Juan and don Genaro left the world.

And since they were around anyway, they did have their occasional uses. Don Juan used one of his once to give Castaneda a taste of what it was like to come into physical contact with one. He did what the old seers used to do to make it materialize itself before Castaneda's eyes. The old seers discovered that what energized their allies the most was animal fear. By doling out their energy in short bursts of fear, the allies would materialize in whatever awesome form that the perceiver projected on them. For example, when the nagual Julian made one of his allies materialize itself before don Juan, don Juan saw it as a monstrous man with the head of a fish with one large green eye in the middle of its forehead. Castaneda saw don Juan and don Genaro's allies as 1) a huge rectangular shadow that crushed anything in its path; 2) as a tall, thin man with bizarre clothing and a bad case of eczema; 3) as a large and vicious coyote; 4) as a big and scary saber-toothed tiger. Maria Elena saw them as mean-looking Indian men who would wait for her in lonely places.

The peculiarities of their individual personalities gave the allies their form.

The allies also made excellent guardians. Don Juan used one to guard his house. Once when Castaneda went to don Juan's house when he was not at home, Castaneda felt a threatening presence that made him leave hastily. Who knows what might have happened to him if he had stayed and his fear became powerful enough to make the ally materialize.

Occasionally don Juan would use his allies to keep a wayward apprentice in line. Lydia, Josefina and Maria Elena were each affected by them when don Juan decided that their personalities were badly flawed.

Don Juan could use his allies only because he was an impeccable and detached nagual. The allies would have drained the energy of anyone who did not have these qualities, leaving them badly injured or dead.

In his first book Castaneda quoted don Juan as saying that his allies were jimson weed and the smoking mixture that contained psychoactive mushrooms. But this was Castaneda's misinterpretation of don Juan's intentions. Don Juan meant that those plant preparations enabled one to make contact with inorganic beings. Indeed, Castaneda's first face-to-face contact with an ally came as a result of smoking don Juan's mix of herbs and hallucinogenic mushrooms. This might seem to contradict the assertion that one could only visit the world of the inorganic beings with their cooperation, but the fact is that the inorganic beings send scouts into the dreams of those attempting to increase the scope of their awareness. And being under the influence of the mushroom mixture could certainly be described as a dream state and as a bid for increased awareness.

19. Why the Warrior's Way? And Why Now?

"The old seers *saw* that the earth has a cocoon. They *saw* that there is a ball encasing the earth, a luminous cocoon that entraps the Eagle's emanations. The earth is a gigantic sentient being subjected to the same forces we are." They considered the earth to be the ultimate source of everything we are. The old seers were not mistaken in this respect, because the earth is indeed our ultimate source." (7,13,205)

Whether we wish to face it or not, we are headed for a very dark future. Overpopulation, pollution and war threaten the existence of nearly all life on this planet. Only the Warrior's Way offers sufficient incentive to turn mankind from its current mode of living. The chance to sustain our consciousness and awareness for millions and perhaps billions of years until the Earth itself dies is an offer too good to resist. The alternative is suffering on a scale so vast as to defy the imagination. It is my personal belief that the Earth (a living, sentient being with an awareness of its own) will not acquiesce to its own destruction and that it will take whatever steps are necessary to ensure its survival. These could include massive earthquakes, tsunamis or the sudden emergence of new bacterial or viral strains. The disappearance of the dinosaurs from Earth is often theorized to have resulted from Earth's collision with a massive asteroid. It is assumed, of course, that such an event was random. That assumption is specious and unwarranted. It does not take into account the possibility that the Earth itself intentionally willed such a collision in order to protect itself from the destructive effects of predatory creatures.

Mankind itself has put in place several mechanisms that could ensure the destruction of most of humanity. Scientists have created weapons for germ warfare that could decimate Earth's population if these bacteria or virus strains should ever escape the rather flimsy confines of the labs in which they were created. One fire or earthquake could result in their escape and the resulting destruction of most of mankind.

Agriculture's increasing dependence on genetically engineered plants, every one of which is genetically identical, renders the food supply susceptible to new forms of bacterial or insect life that could destroy every one of these identical plants. The resulting famine and the inevitable wars over the remaining food supplies would be cataclysmic.

The seers of the Warrior's Way have informed us that the meaning of, the reason for life is the enhancement of consciousness. All living things have consciousness, an awareness of the experience of life. The fact that we have no way of perceiving, measuring or experiencing that consciousness in species other than our own is irrelevant. If one particular species threatens that process for most living beings, that species will undoubtedly be dealt with in whatever manner is necessary to prevent further damage. It is a very stark choice. Either mankind transfers its energy and awareness to the Third Attention, or it will be completely destroyed or decimated to such an extent that it no longer threatens itself or other life forms. The reason that mankind is offered the chance to experience the Third Attention is to continue the process of enhancing and enriching awareness but without damaging the chance of other living beings to enhance theirs, as we are doing now.

Our present and perilous situation requires that we evolve much faster than physical evolution can occur. That leaves only one possibility—to expand and explore the possibilities of enhanced perception and awareness.

It is certainly not my intention to drive people to the Warrior's Way through fear, as that will accomplish nothing. I am constantly reminded of the truth of don Juan's statement that people love to be told what to do, but they love even more not doing what they are told. People have to convinced that following the warrior's path is in their own best interest. Nothing else will move them. But I would be remiss if I did not honestly state the situation, as I see it, that faces all of us.

No true warrior will ever come to your door to convince, coerce or trick you into accepting the Warrior's Way. Each person must come to the Warrior's Way of their own accord. It is true that in the past a nagual (the leader of a party of warriors) would often use fear and trickery to induce prospective apprentices to come to the warrior's path, but that is an entirely different situation than the one we face now. To lead the masses of people to accept the Warrior's Way will require total honesty, discipline and commitment on the part of the new leadership that is coming. There is nothing easy about the Warrior's Way. It requires a level of discipline that is, unfortunately, quite alien to the indulgent lifestyles that so many of us lead now.

Since the publication of Castaneda's first book in 1968, an army of charlatans, would-be shamans, and pop philosophers have emerged with purely commercial intent. They harvest a few of the kernels of wisdom offered by don Juan and use them to convince people that transcendence is possible without doing the work involved. The Warrior's Way is all or nothing at all! There are no shortcuts! One cannot pick and choose among the techniques that the Warrior's Way offers for conserving energy. All of them must be practiced tirelessly or one's progression will be negligible. The Warrior's Way was meant to change the course of human history, not to amuse self-indulgent dabblers in mysticism or make them more comfortable in their materialistic misery.

The End of History is in no way meant to be a substitute for the careful study of the words of don Juan as reported in the books of Carlos Castaneda. It was written to be a reintroduction to, and an overview of, the Warrior's Way's most basic concepts and as a response to the cynical distortions inflicted upon the Warrior's Way by the media. And to make it clear that we received the Warrior's Way through a cracked lens–filtered through Castaneda's tragically flawed personality. It is the words of don Juan that matter. Nothing else.

Don Juan was a man, not a myth! He walked among us!

20. The Life of Don Juan Matus

Don Juan Matus was born in Yuma, Arizona in 1891. His father was a Yaqui Indian from Sonora, Mexico. His mother was a Yuma Indian from Arizona. The exact circumstances under which his father came to live in Arizona are not known, but there is a distinct possibility that he was in exile after the Battle of El Anil in 1886, which ended the short-lived Yaqui republic established in Sonora by 4,000 Yaqui under the leadership of Cajeme (Jose Maria Peres). After this battle most of the Yaqui towns near the Rio Yaqui were abandoned and the residents fled north to Arizona.

The Yaqui had been fighting the Spanish and the Mexicans since 1740, and hostilities did not finally cease until 1929, when the Mexican government placed military garrisons at all Yaqui settlements. In 1897 a peace treaty was signed between the Yaquis and the Mexican government but armed conflict resumed in 1899. It was around this time that don Juan's family returned to Sonora, presumably so that his father could assist the badly outnumbered and outgunned Yaqui.

Whatever the exact reason, their return to Sonora ended tragically. One day when don Juan's father was away, Mexican soldiers came upon their camp and killed don Juan's mother as he watched. When he tried to hold on to his mother's body, the soldiers broke one of his hands with a horsewhip, beat him, and dragged him away. He was put on a prisoner train headed for exile in southern Mexico. "For days they kept us there in the dark, like animals. They kept us alive with bits of food they threw into the wagon from time to time." He found his father, badly wounded, on the same train. But they were not to be reunited for long. "My father died of his wounds in that wagon. He became delirious with pain and fever and went on telling me that I had to survive. He went on telling me that until the very last moment of his life."

After his father's death, don Juan, already a skinny child, was kept from starvation by the other prisoners, who made sure that he got enough food to survive the trip. Another prisoner, an old woman curer, set the bones of his broken hand. After arriving in the southern Mexican state of Yucatan he managed to locate some relatives who cared for him. But life was still very hard for him and his fellow Yaqui exiles. Those who were not enslaved worked for little pay in the tobacco plantations of Yucatan.

Not only did don Juan live with the memory of witnessing the deaths of both of his parents, he also lived with the constant threat of starvation. "To be very hungry was the only thing I knew as a child, and I used to swell up until I could not breathe ...." Before his father's death don Juan had promised him that he would someday destroy his killers and this promise haunted him for many years. The bitterness of those memories led him to become an aggressive, mean and wild young man with a terrible temper. He hated the Mexicans and hated the humble attitude that Mexican employers required of their Indian workers. He received no formal education. But despite all this he managed to work hard and to become very strong.

By the time he was twenty years old he was working in a sugar mill doing heavy physical labor. One day he was at work moving large sacks of sugar when he was noticed by a well-dressed woman of means. She had a word with don Juan's foreman, who then approached him with an offer to work at her house for very good money, the only condition being that he pay the foreman for the privilege of getting the job. Don Juan thought himself most fortunate to find such a well-paying job and instantly agreed to the foreman's terms. He was taken to a house far from town and left with his new foreman, an ugly and physically imposing man who began questioning him about various subjects. When don Juan told him that he had no family, his new foreman was very pleased. He told don Juan that he would be making lots of money and would be fed and housed on the premises, and could even begin saving money. But then the foreman began to laugh at him in a way that scared don Juan badly - as if to say, "If you believe this you are unbelievably naive and stupid and will make the perfect victim." But before he could run away, the foreman pulled a gun and forced don Juan to begin working, working harder than he ever had at the most dangerous and exhausting jobs imaginable.

Every day the foreman threatened him with death or imprisonment if he did not continue working himself, literally, to death. Don Juan soon realized that he had become a victim of a con game in which the two foremen brought Indians to the house, worked them to death and then divided the salaries the victims were never given a chance to spend. After three weeks in these hellish conditions don Juan had the temerity to request some time off to pay the sugar mill foreman some of the money that he owed to him. That was when his new foreman made it very clear that don Juan would never leave the house alive; he would be worked until he died just like the Indian he had replaced. Upon hearing that his fate was sealed, don Juan was overcome by a burst of anger and ran into the house and out the front door, yelling his head off. The foreman was momentarily caught off guard but managed to catch up with him on the road in front of the house, where he shot him once in the chest and left him for dead. He would have shot him again to make sure that he was finished off but he was bumped into by an old Indian who was passing by on the road with his wife. There were several other spectators around also, so the foreman left.

The old man who had prevented don Juan's certain death was the nagual Julian, who happened to be looking for an apprentice nagual. When he saw don Juan lying there badly wounded he realized that don Juan had the perfect energy configuration to become his new apprentice. And three omens had indicated that don Juan was the man. First was a small cyclone of wind that raised a cloud of dust near where Don Juan was lying; second was the fact that the thought of needing a new apprentice nagual had crossed nagual Julian's mind just before he heard the shot that wounded don Juan; the third was bumping into the foreman before he could shoot don Juan again.

Realizing that he had to act fast because don Juan was literally bleeding to death, nagual Julian immediately cried out, "They've shot my son!" Discretely signaling his female companion, a seer who played the role in public of his wife, to play along, they both went into hysterics, crying over don Juan's body. They persuaded some husky young men who were on the scene to help them carry the unconscious don Juan to a house that the nagual Julian kept in a city some distance away.

When he regained consciousness and found himself being tended to by an old man who called himself Belisario, and his fat, disagreeable wife, don Juan didn't know what to think. He thought that they were very kind to do what they had done for him but resolved to steal away when healed enough to do so. He, of course, had no idea who he was dealing with. The nagual Julian was a consummate actor who had, before becoming a nagual, actually worked as a theatre professional. Not only could he fool anyone, but he also had the power to move his assemblage point in ways that would alter his appearance totally. There were several guises that he could assume on a moment's notice; a fat man, a skinny old man with rheumatism, a handsome young man; he could even physically become a woman. Don Juan never had a chance.

Having sensed don Juan's plan to escape at the first opportunity, the nagual Julian waited until he was almost healed and then made one of the inorganic beings that he kept as an ally burst into the room where don Juan lay. The ally had assumed the form of a monstrous one-eyed giant who scared don Juan so badly that he fainted. When he came to he was told that the monster was their master and had enslaved them in that house as his servants. To attempt escape was futile, as they would be caught and killed in the most horrible way possible. The nagual said their only hope was if they could somehow eventually come up with a foolproof plan to escape but until that day, their fates were sealed. Overwhelmed and scared stiff by the sight of that monstrous man, don Juan lapsed into depression and compliance. Every so often the nagual Julian would make the monster reappear to reinforce his fear, so don Juan did not try to escape.

When he was fully healed, the nagual gave him another, different jolt of fear and uncertainty. One day he announced that the monster had left for a few days and that he no longer had to maintain the disguise he used to fool their master. Jumping up with a younger man's agility, he dipped his head into a container of water for a moment and when he pulled his head out he had become a handsome man who looked to be in his thirties. Don Juan, believing the nagual to be the devil, was sure that he was done for. He was even more surprised when he was asked to wait outside on the front porch so that the young man could make love to his wife, who, the nagual said, was disguised as an older fat woman but was really young and beautiful. So don Juan waited outside as the young man and his wife shook the house with their lovemaking. After the house had become still don Juan re-entered to find the nagual gone but found his beautiful young wife (actually a different woman from the nagual's party) sleeping naked on their bed. Having never seen a beautiful woman naked before he was overcome with embarrassment and when he heard what he thought to be the monstrous man returning, he passed out with fear. When he regained consciousness, the nagual had resumed being an old man and his wife was again fat and very ill-tempered.

All during this time the nagual Julian would often force don Juan into heightened awareness and begin his instruction as an apprentice nagual. But since don Juan could not remember having being taught anything when he returned to his normal awareness, he remained frightened and confused.

Then one day don Juan saw that Belisario and his wife were packing their things to leave and was informed that they had made a deal with the monstrous man. They were to be given their freedom in exchange for bringing don Juan to the house to be the monstrous man's new slave. After apologizing for leaving him behind, the nagual Julian assured him that things would not be that bad. If don Juan behaved well he would survive. If not, he would die. Desperate and struck numb with terror, don Juan asked if there was anything that he could do to escape his predicament. The nagual replied that he and his wife were going to the state of Durango to learn sorcery to make sure that the monster could never pursue and enslave them again. He asked don Juan if he would consider learning sorcery and don Juan said, "I am an Indian. I was born to hate and fear witches."

And so the nagual and his companion left don Juan sitting on the porch. He could hear the monster banging around inside the house as if waiting impatiently for his return. He was so convulsed with fear that he vomited. He sat there for hours unable to leave, or go back inside the house, or even move. Then he looked up and saw the old man trying to get his attention from across the street. Belisario crawled with excruciating slowness across the street until he reached don Juan and told him that he felt so bad about leaving him behind that he had returned, despite his wife's objections, to try to rescue him. Having previously told don Juan that the monster had very bad eyesight, he told him to go back in the house and change into a disguise. He then handed don Juan a bundle of clothes to wear. Not until he had gone back inside did he discover that the bundle contained women's clothing. Disgusted by the very thought of wearing women's clothing, he almost gave up until he heard the sounds of the monstrous man growling in another room. Then his fear at being left behind overruled his objections to wearing women's clothes and he put them on.

As he left the house the nagual, who had learned to disguise his laughter by appearing to weep, began to cry as if his heart would break. He guided don Juan to where his wife and two muleteers were waiting with a wagon and they left the city. The nagual told don Juan that the monster would eventually discover he was missing and might pursue them at any moment, so he would have to stay in his disguise for the entire trip. And he would have to pretend to be a woman and be good enough at it to fool even the muleteers. Don Juan didn't realize it at the time, but his disguise was not just for the nagual Julian's amusement. By being forced to wear women's clothing he was being taught a lesson about the injustice of women's subservient place in society (this was in 1911), but also about the superior ability of women in the art of *stalking*.

When the nagual tried to speak to him directly about *stalking* don Juan ignored him, and being so humiliated by the idea of having to pretend to be a woman, asked for some men's clothes so that he could take his chances on his own. But soon after he had left the nagual's party the monstrous man/beast appeared out of nowhere and began chasing him. Realizing he had no choice, he bolted back to the wagon and put on his disguise for the rest of the journey.

After traveling for a month they reached Durango and the old man took don Juan to a large hacienda where he was told he could hide out and be safe from his pursuer. Then he left. Don Juan was greeted by seven beautiful women and one unfriendly man who appeared to have nothing to say to him. The women treated him kindly and were fascinated by don Juan's disguise and his tale of being chased by a monstrous one-eyed man. A few days later one of the women gave him some men's clothes and told him that since the monster, which the others in the household said they had never seen, was no longer around, he was free to leave. But don Juan had seen the monster lurking in the bushes around the hacienda and begged to be allowed to stay. He was then told that he could stay but could ask no questions and would be expected to do whatever was asked of him. Feeling he had no choice, don Juan agreed to these terms.

A few weeks later the young man who don Juan thought had disguised himself as Belisario showed up at the hacienda. The young man introduced himself, saying that his name was Julian and that he was the owner of the hacienda. When don Juan queried him about his disguise, Belisario, and the monster, the young man emphatically stated that he knew nothing of any disguise or monster. He said that he knew Belisario and would allow don Juan to stay as a favor to the old man since don Juan obviously felt the need to hide from whatever had scared him. Thoroughly embarrassed, don Juan reminded Julian that they had met. But the nagual said that he had never seen don Juan before that day and had no idea what don Juan was talking about.

Then the young man stated that as the master of the house he was in charge of everyone in it, including don Juan and that if don Juan did not like it he was free to leave at any time. After asking what would be expected of him, don Juan was led by the young man to a section of the house still under construction and told that it was symbolic of the role that he was expected to play. "You are one of the elements of that incomplete construction," he said to don Juan. "Let's say that you are the beam that will support the roof. Until we put it in place and put the roof on top of it, we don't know whether it will support the weight. The master carpenter says it will. I am the master carpenter."

Confused, don Juan asked exactly what he was expected to do in terms of work, so the nagual took another tack. "I'm a nagual," he said. "I bring freedom. Without my intervention, there is no way to freedom." Hearing these words, don Juan began to wonder about the nagual's soundness of mind. He knew what the word nagual meant, but was preoccupied with knowing exactly what his own duties would be.

Seeing that he was not getting through to don Juan, the nagual then explained that don Juan would be his assistant and personal valet. He would not be paid for these duties but would occasionally be given special chores for which he would be paid, and so would have a little money should he ever decide to leave. There were also three requirements for his stay. First, he had to learn everything the women of the household might decide to teach him. Second, his conduct and behavior must be above reproach at all times. Third, he must address the young man as nagual and only call him the nagual Julian when speaking about him to others.

Don Juan accepted the nagual's demands because he had no choice, but was not happy about it. He sulked and said barely a word to anyone. His bad attitude became so apparent that the nagual Julian called the entire household together and asked them to vote on whether the ill-tempered young man should be allowed to stay. The women all voted no, but the nagual began to act as if he had sympathy for don Juan. He argued that if don Juan really saw a monster that that could be the reason he was always so worried and sulky. A loud argument broke out among them, but don Juan barely heard them. He was convinced that he would be forced out and that the monster would take him back into captivity. He began to cry. His tears softened the attitude of some of the women and an alternative was proposed. After a three week probationary period, his attitude would be reevaluated. If his behavior was not exemplary, he must leave.

After an agreement had been reached, the nagual pulled don Juan aside and told him that he could see the monster but could not admit it to the others. He said that don Juan had better behave himself or that he would be at the mercy of the monstrous man. So knowing he had no choice, don Juan altered his behavior so that he might stay.

He remained at the hacienda for three years during which he was taught to read, write and keep the nagual's account books. He even agreed to learn sorcery in order to overcome the monster that kept him there as a virtual prisoner. But although the nagual Julian talked with him often, he seemed most interested in pulling pranks on him. Don Juan became convinced that no one at the hacienda actually knew or practiced sorcery.

What he did not understand was the nagual Julian's teaching method. The nagual was not given to explanations. Being a master *stalker*, he would never state his intentions directly when his apprentices were in their normal state of awareness. He would beat around the bush and speak only in a very general way about the topic at hand. Then he would move the assemblage points of his apprentices through strange and sometimes rather brutal pranks so that the apprentice could reach a realization, to claim knowledge on his own.

But don Juan had not yet claimed any knowledge that he was aware of, since he couldn't remember any of the nagual's teachings that had been given to him in heightened awareness. The nagual had begun to teach him the basics of *stalking* and *dreaming*. And had made him begin a recapitulation of his life. But, as a practical man, don Juan could see little use for these things. "I didn't know that I was storing power when I first began to learn the ways of a warrior," he said to Castaneda much later. "Just like you, I thought I wasn't doing anything in particular, but that was not so. Power has the peculiarity of being unnoticeable when it is being stored."

One thing that don Juan did understand was the nagual's promise that someday don Juan would have the beautiful women of his party for his own and that he would make him rich beyond imagination. He tricked don Juan with enticements that were meant to appeal to the weakest parts of his character, his sensual desires and his greed.

But after three years don Juan had unknowingly stored enough personal power to confront the monstrous man. One day he found himself facing that horrendous being, advancing on him, until the nagual's ally faded away into thin air. But instead of being pleased with his success in this battle of power, he reverted to his old hot-tempered self and became very angry.

He called all the members of the house together, including the nagual, and berated them for tricking him with a monster that did not exist. All along he had felt that he was being exploited and the realization that he had worked for years for nearly nothing because of a trick enraged him even more. The women, who had known what was really happening all along, began to laugh their heads off. Nagual Julian, while crying uncontrollably, apologized for lying. But don Juan would have none of it. He demanded to be paid his savings. Feeling humiliated and betrayed, he left without saying goodbye.

At first elated to be on his own, he soon rediscovered that life outside the sheltered environment of the nagual's house was hard, very hard indeed. Traveling was complicated and costly. But he had a hunger for new experiences. Having never had sex, he was eager to try it, even though the nagual had told him that his strength and endurance were the result of having never been with a woman. He left from a nearby city for the port of Mazatlan with two muleteers and by the time he arrived there he was an experienced muleteer himself. He was offered a job driving a mule train on a regular route between Mazatlan and Durango, but a mysterious desire to go north made him refuse the offer and take whatever jobs he could find as headed there.

He ended up in the state of Sinaloa, where he found himself playing the role of surrogate husband and father to a young widow and her family. Becoming their protector and breadwinner was a new and difficult job, and slowly his energy began to wane. For years he struggled to feed and clothe them, but his luck at finding jobs, so strong at first, began to fade away as time passed by. He worked relentlessly from dawn to dusk but could make no real progress beyond their bare, meager existence.

Then one day he awoke in his bed unable to move, paralyzed. It was if his body was telling him that he had to rest and would not move until he had done so. As he lay there he began to look back on the events that had brought him to this pass. And then he realized that he had erred in believing that the nagual and his party were merely abusing him. Then he knew that the nagual had been his only hope of ever attaining freedom and that he had thoughtlessly thrown away his chance to be with them. Not long after this realization, his paralysis ended as mysteriously as it had begun and he resumed his attempts to provide for his family. But still he made no progress.

Eventually he lost all hope and began to believe that death would soon overtake him. Day after day he sat outside his hut with his wife and children and recapitulated his life completely.

Then he had a stroke of luck, or so he believed. He was hired as a temporary fieldworker for the harvest. But one day his hat was stolen. Unable to work in the hot sun without one, he covered his head with straw and rags. When the other workers saw his hat, they began to laugh at him. Their taunts and laughter escalated to such a pitch that the foreman became alarmed. Afraid that they would begin arguing and fighting among themselves, the foreman fired don Juan.

Consumed with righteous anger, don Juan sat at the edge of the field crying and cursing his fate. He realized then that he had lost the chance for freedom offered by the nagual Julian, had thrown away his only hope of ever escaping the poverty and ignorance that claims the lives of so many. And there, on the edge of that field, he died.

But the spirit had other things in mind for him. Accepting his recapitulation as a substitute for his life and awareness, it sent him back to the world to try again. After seeming to be dead for at least a day, he awoke to find himself buried in a shallow grave. After digging himself out, he went to find his wife and her children, but they were gone. They had already heard that he was dead and had moved on, vanished.

So, after five and a half years away, he returned to the nagual Julian, who treated him as if he had never been gone. Resuming his apprenticeship, he realized that it had taken his death to convince him that he truly was a warrior, a warrior who could no longer share the world of ordinary people and who had to find a new path in a world of mystery.

Returning to the nagual Julian's house and his apprenticeship, however, was no bed of ease. The nagual could often be a unyielding and terrifying master. "Naguals are not really the most friendly beings on earth," don Juan said later. "I learned this the hard way, being pitted against my teacher, the terrible nagual Julian. His mere presence used to scare the daylights out of me. And when he used to zero in on me, I always thought my life wasn't worth a plug nickel."

Fortunately for don Juan, nagual Julian's benefactor, the nagual Elias, had not yet left the world and took a strong hand in don Juan's instruction, buffering the impact of the nagual Julian's fearsome nature. "It was the luckiest thing that could have happened to me, for I had the opportunity to be taught by two opposite temperaments. It was like being reared by a powerful father and an even more powerful grandfather who don't see eye to eye. In such a contest, the grandfather always wins."

The nagual Julian was not given to explanations, but the nagual Elias was. The nagual Julian was loud and extroverted while the nagual Elias was quiet and somber. When don Juan felt under siege from the nagual Julian's harshness, he could visit and talk with the nagual Elias. At the nagual Elias' request, don Juan lived with him for six years. Don Juan enjoyed the peace and solace he found with the nagual Elias, but was often bored in his house, for which he felt very guilty. The nagual Julian's high energy and his ability as a raconteur were endlessly entertaining. The pranks that he would pull had the appeal of high drama. "His dramas were always bigger than life. I assure you we didn't know what enjoyment was until we saw what he did when some of those dramas backfired on him."

But the two naguals were never in disagreement about the behavior expected of the apprentices or the goals set for them. They differed only in the most practical and effective methods of reaching those goals. They were both very clear, for instance, when they told the apprentices that they must conserve their sexual energy and teamed up to give them a direct demonstration of its importance. One day, with no warning, they created an opening to the Third Attention and shoved them all inside. The apprentices nearly died there because they had not followed the naguals' demand that they conserve their sexual energy. The one apprentice who had followed the naguals' instructions, Silvio Manuel, was the only one not affected.

That incident was not the only example of don Juan's failure to follow directions. After being told by the nagual Julian that he should avoid archaeological sites and artifacts created by the old seers, particularly the pyramids at Tula, don Juan practically lived there. As a result he attracted the attention of a group of old seers and their allies. They followed don Juan home and jumped on him in an attempt to feast on his energy by scaring him to death. The nagual Julian had to take quick action to rescue don Juan or he would have been done for. He "buried" don Juan in a dirt coffin (a wooden frame the size of a coffin covered with dirt) that he kept ready behind the house. He was kept there until the phantoms gave up and left. Don Juan was so scared that he used to sleep in it for a long time after the danger had passed.

After securing don Juan as his apprentice nagual, the nagual Julian began to gather other apprentices for don Juan's party. He saw that don Juan did not yet have enough power to gather them on his own. The usual order of events called for finding a nagual woman first, then four female seers, then four male seers. The nagual Julian asked the women of his party to secure the four women seers for don Juan's party. When he heard of this plan, don Juan was fascinated by the possibility of having four women for, as he understood it, his own personal use in whatever manner he chose, namely sexual use.

Before that could happen don Juan had to meet the warriors of the nagual's party. The first two he met were two female warriors who were the most massive Indian women he had ever seen. They hated him on sight, beating him up and then throwing him on the ground and sitting on him for twelve hours while his benefactor negotiated with them for his release. After they finally relented, don Juan was immediately taken to meet the other members of the nagual's party, who didn't think much more of him than the first two had. They said he was too stupid and wild to be a successful nagual, and once again the nagual Julian had to intercede on his behalf.

He was then placed under the supervision of the two fiercest female seers of the nagual's party. They saw that don Juan did not have the detachment to deal with female seers without his mind being clouded by lustful thoughts, so they changed the order of events and set about first finding four male warriors for his group. In the meantime, to cure don Juan of his lust, they kept him suspended in a leather harness from the ceiling of their kitchen. He spent most of his time that way for six months as the warriors of the nagual's group searched for the members for his group. The combination of the cleansing effect of being suspended in the harness and his interaction with the members of the nagual's party did eventually have the desired effect. They began to bring out the qualities that would make don Juan a leader, a true nagual.

As the other apprentices began to arrive, don Juan was underwhelmed by their personalities. Hearing the stories about their lives before coming to the nagual's hacienda, don Juan at first thought that they were a pathetic lot. However, he soon became friends with one of the other apprentices, Vicente Medrano. Vicente, the nagual Julian's first apprentice, was a herbalist who specialized in making preparations from the medicinal plants that he and don Juan gathered in the mountains. They both sold plants and potions in the market in Oaxaca when they were still in their twenties, loudly singing out the virtues and healing abilities of their wares to attract the attention of potential customers.

But the nagual Julian was constantly after don Juan to be friends with all the new male and female apprentices. Since he thought so little of them, he often ended up laughing at them for being so gullible as to fall under the influence of the nagual and told them that they were being exploited ruthlessly. He believed that he was smarter than them all and could see exactly what his benefactor was doing to them.

To encourage a sense of camaraderie and group spirit, the nagual often took them into the mountains and left them there under don Juan's supervision. The nagual told them that he wanted them to find the spirit, but his efforts were in vain. Don Juan, however, became preoccupied with the thought of knowing the spirit. And the nagual encouraged him relentlessly to go after it, again in vain. He began to argue with his benefactor about the possibility of relating to something so vague and ephemeral, until at last the nagual promised to give him a lesson that would not only show him what the spirit was, but also how to explain it.

To celebrate don Juan's lesson, the nagual decided to hold a big party on the banks of a rushing river swollen to flood stage by heavy rain. The members of the household ate, drank, staged skits and enjoyed themselves immensely. When the fun was over, the nagual asked if any of the others would like to be a part of don Juan's lesson. Knowing the unpredictability of the nagual Julian and his sometimes brutal tactics, they all said no.

So the nagual took don Juan to the edge of the rushing river and told him to kneel. He then began a long and ridiculous incantation asking the river to teach don Juan the spirit. Then he picked don Juan up and threw him in, saying, "Don't hate the river, for heaven's sake!"

To say that don Juan was surprised would be an understatement. Astonished would better a better word to describe his feelings. Then he became angry and resolved not to drown because of the nagual's mercilessness. As the river tumbled him around he began to dog-paddle in an attempt to merely stay afloat. And a strange feeling came over him. He realized that he had always been a very angry man, but that anger would not help in this situation at all. He could not hate or fight the river. He could only be caught in its flow and try to survive.

That sudden change of feelings, combined with his desperate attempt to stay alive, caused his assemblage point to move. Somehow he found himself running alongside the river, watching himself trying not to drown. The free movement of his assemblage point had split him in two. One don Juan was trying merely to survive the raging river while another part of himself ran alongside the river watching. He began to alternate the sensations of one moment being in the river and the next running beside it.

At last, several miles downstream, he managed to pull himself out of the river on the opposite shore. He stayed there for over a week while waiting for the river to subside, remaining in his double state the whole time. He found that he could be one or the other and that his new double had extraordinary abilities. It could travel long distances instantly; it could find food and shelter.

After a time he used that part of himself to travel back to the nagual's house to see if the others were concerned about his fate. He was curious to find out what they really thought of him. But as he watched them, the nagual noticed his presence and put an end to his game. Appearing out of nowhere as a black, bell-shaped object of tremendous strength, he seized don Juan in a excruciatingly painful grip.

Immediately he found himself back by the river and, seeing that it had receded, crossed over and headed back. But on his way he decided to stop first at the nagual Elias' house to seek an explanation of what had happened. The nagual Elias told him that his benefactor's actions resulted in a movement of the assemblage point that enabled him to experience silent knowledge, to experience the spirit directly. And that showed don Juan he could experience either position of the assemblage point, its usual position or the position that enabled him to know the spirit.

The nagual Elias was very excited that don Juan had managed to transfer all his energy from one point to the other and kept that ability for days. He said it demonstrated a prodigious ability to move his assemblage point that boded well for don Juan's future as a nagual.

One apprentice the nagual Julian was particularly on the lookout for was a nagual woman. A nagual woman is the male nagual's counterpart and soul mate. Traditionally she enters the Third Attention with the male nagual's benefactor's party. The male nagual's desire to be reunited with her is a powerful incentive to complete the task of preparing himself and his own party to reach the Third Attention.

Eventually the nagual Julian did find a nagual woman, Olinda, the daughter of some prosperous merchants who lived in the nearby town. But he did not tell don Juan of this development directly. He decided to arrange that they meet and then let don Juan take the necessary steps to secure her. To this end the nagual Julian suddenly began to attend church, insisting that don Juan accompany him. Don Juan was not comfortable with the social interaction required when attending church and thought that the nagual was trying to teach him to be more at ease in these situations. His benefactor had told him that this ability was very important for a nagual. At one service don Juan found himself kneeling next to a young woman named Olinda. When their eyes met, don Juan knew that she was the nagual woman. They were both instantly overwhelmed by the depth of their feelings for each other.

The nagual, having completed his task of bringing them together, rose from his seat and immediately left the church, attracting the attention of all the other parishioners, who turned to watch. Don Juan, feeling that he should leave with the nagual, tried to go but Olinda grabbed his hand and stopped him.

After the service was over, don Juan found his benefactor outside the church trying to comfort Olinda's family, who were scandalized by the public display of affection between them. They felt that don Juan was not a suitable match for their daughter and were opposed to any relationship between them.

At this point don Juan was at a loss as to how to proceed. The nagual told him that he had to do whatever was necessary, even if it meant marrying her against her parents' wishes. He said that he could assist don Juan only if Olinda went with him willingly.

So don Juan, with the assistance of Silvio Manuel, concocted an elaborate plot to kidnap Olinda. He and don Juan disguised themselves as washerwomen and entered Olinda's home unnoticed carrying a large bundle of clothes. Stealing into her room, Silvio Manuel used his mesmeric powers to make her faint. They then took her out the back door wrapped up so that it looked as if they were taking out dirty laundry. But after having taken her to the hacienda, their benefactor reminded them that the nagual woman must come willingly, not by force. So Silvio Manuel altered their plan to make it appear that don Juan was rescuing her from the kidnappers. The rescue, during which don Juan had to pretend to have been badly injured, was planned to take place near the nagual Julian's hacienda so that Olinda would willingly help the "injured" don Juan into the house. Once she did so, the nagual Julian put her into heightened awareness and secured her allegiance to the warrior's path.

By the end of his apprenticeship, don Juan was an expert at the identification, preparation and use of three different power plants, peyote (Lophophora williamsii), Jimson weed ("the devil's weed")(Datura inoxia syn. D. meteloides) and a hallucinogenic mushroom (possibly Psylilocybe mexicana). Of the three he preferred chewing peyote or smoking an herbal mixture containing the psychoactive mushroom. Jimson weed gave him a strange, almost supernatural vigor. "I killed a man with a single blow of my arm. I could toss boulders, huge boulders not even twenty men could budge. Once I jumped so high I chopped the leaves off the highest trees." But trying to use Jimson weed gave him fits. "The devil's weed nearly killed me every time I tried to use her. Once it was so bad I thought I was finished."

He associated Jimson weed with the obstreperous personality of the nagual Julian. "My benefactor was given to shouting, and to all the clatter and violence of the devil's weed." Peyote and the mushroom mixture he associated with the more contemplative nature of the nagual Elias, whose personality he felt was closer to his own.

The uses of these power plants were legacies of the old seers, who used Jimson weed and the mushroom mixture to put them into contact with allies, inorganic beings. His benefactor, at don Juan's request, gave him an example of another way the old seers contacted them.

He had don Juan build a mirror with a wooden frame. Together they submerged it in a shallow stream. As they gazed into it through the water an inorganic being appeared in it. And then, attracted by their energy—particularly don Juan's fear and wonder at such a sight—it came out of the mirror. At this point in the demonstration they were supposed to have simply removed the mirror from the water to keep the ally from emerging, but the inorganic being's ferocious pull made the mirror break, so it was able to come out. It began chasing don Juan, who ran as if pursued by the devil.

His benefactor shouted to him to stay in the area until he could build a fire and use its flames to shield him from the ally, so don Juan began to run in circles. Don Juan began to suspect that the nagual Julian was secretly enjoying his plight and was going about the business of making the fire in a rather leisurely way, and he became very angry with the nagual. He became so angry that he even stopped for a moment and yelled at his benefactor for putting him in such a spot, until he noticed the nagual looking past him in horror at the inorganic being looming over them both.

Running in circles again, he heard his benefactor go into a long explanation that it would take time to build a fire big enough and that the tactic might not work, excuses that don Juan believed he was making to prolong his enjoyment of the situation. But he kept running and running, seemingly for hours.

At last the fire was built and the nagual's plan worked. They stayed by the fire all night but near dawn the ally managed to shove an exhausted don Juan into it, burning him badly.

Later don Juan found out what had actually occurred; that inorganic beings can use the energy of men to materialize themselves in this world. That's what it looks like, at least. They are actually only projections of limited energy from their own world, but the energy of men makes them more vigorous. That is the method used to make them seem to materialize in this world.

Don Juan's *dreaming* practices also put him in touch with the inorganic beings so that he could absorb the energy of their world. The inorganic beings allow selected *dreamers* to visit their world in an attempt to persuade them to live there. But don Juan found them repulsive and subsequently dealt with them only as necessary. He was after freedom, not the slavery that imprisoned the old seers.

That did not stop him, however, from making use of the two allies he inherited from his benefactor. For instance, he used one of them to guard his house from intruders.

After his benefactor left the world to enter the Third Attention, don Juan inherited not only his allies, but also his assets; namely the very valuable hacienda. But instead of maintaining it and assuming the guise of a wealthy landowner, as the nagual Julian had, don Juan sold it and invested the money in stocks and bonds. As a stockholder don Juan was required to meet occasionally with brokers and bankers. On these occasions he wore custom tailored suits that transformed his appearance totally. Usually he wore khaki pants, a khaki shirt, homemade sandals and a straw hat. But for his business appointments he wore a three piece suit, dress shirt, tie and dress shoes, his hair neatly combed.

During his time in the nagual Julian's house, don Juan had developed a love for reading and read everything he could get his hands on. He could speak superb Spanish. And so when dealing with his business contacts he presented the image of a sophisticated urban dweller.

He regularly went to Mexico City on business trips and usually stayed at the hotel del Prado, in the Paseo Alameda. He often dined at the Cafe Tacuba, a well-known restaurant in downtown Mexico City. He is not known to have owned a car himself and was driven to his appointments in the city by associates or by Castaneda after they had met in 1960.

He set up four different households for himself and the members of his party in various parts of Mexico. His main house was located somewhere in the mountainous region near Oaxaca. He had a home in Arizona and also maintained a very modest dwelling in Sonora, about one hundred miles south of the city of Guaymas, where Castaneda found him after their first meeting at the Greyhound bus station in Nogales, Arizona.

When Carlos Castaneda first met him, he described don Juan as being five feet nine inches tall with the body of an athlete—his shoulders broad, his stomach flat. His head was round; his hair short and white. Though almost seventy years old, the only real appearance of age was the wrinkles on his face. His dark eyes seemed to glow. His steps were firm but his body agile. He possessed great endurance, being able to walk vigorously for hours in any weather without stopping.

When Castaneda asked him how he maintained his body in such a youthful state don Juan replied, "The secret is not in what you do to yourself but rather in what you don't do." He did not smoke. He drank only water, never alcohol or soda pop. He sometimes chewed peyote buttons during a mitote, or peyote ceremony. But I have the feeling that it was not so much for the effects as for demonstrating his full participation to the others involved. To have such a man among them would undoubtedly inspire confidence.

Despite his admiration for the nagual Julian as a man and master stalker, don Juan disagreed with his teaching method. He saw that merely insinuating knowledge and then waiting for an apprentice to claim it wasted valuable time. And since don Juan did not begin gathering apprentices until he was nearly seventy years old, time was an important consideration. He believed that his patience and verbal dexterity could prepare his apprentices for a movement of the assemblage point that would demonstrate the particular concept he wished to elucidate and also dispel any confusion an apprentice experienced afterwards. It was then up to the student to conserve enough energy to later replicate the movement of the assemblage point don Juan had demonstrated.

He strongly empathized with the difficulty of learning and would often equate himself with his apprentices, saying things like, "You and I are so alike, we are both fools." What he really meant by such statements was that when he was in their position, his confusion and uncertainty were equal or even greater. When Castaneda later realized the absurdity of these reassurances and pointed out the obvious fact that don Juan was far beyond them, don Juan replied, "What you're witnessing is the result of a lifelong struggle. What you see is a warrior who has finally learned to follow the designs of the spirit, but that's all."

He also appreciated the fact that the presence of a commanding teacher often inhibited his apprentices, saying, "I'm sure that it is the nagual's presence that sometimes makes people act dumb. When the Nagual Julian was still around, I was dumber than I am now." He did manage to retain some of his benefactor's flair for the dramatic by ending his meetings with Castaneda on an abrupt note.

One of the legacies from the nagual Julian and the other naguals of his lineage don Juan did not care for at all. That was their relationship with the death defier. The death defier was an old seer from thousands of years ago who had managed to manipulate his assemblage point to sustain his awareness indefinitely. He first came into contact with the nagual Sebastian in 1723. The nagual was going about his duties as the sexton in the cathedral when he confronted by a middle-aged Indian who said he needed some of the nagual's energy. At first the nagual Sebastian tried to act as if he didn't know what the Indian was talking about, but after the death defier threatened to expose him to the church's higher-ups as a sorcerer, he had no choice but to comply with his wishes.

They went into the mountains together and the nagual was gone for several days. When he returned, seemingly none the worse, he had extensive knowledge of the activities and rituals of the ancient seers, courtesy of the death defier. The death defier had learned to manipulate the luminous energy shell of a nagual to release energy that he could use to sustain himself. In exchange he provided information about the old sorcerers and the knowledge necessary for a nagual to attain total perception in selected positions of the assemblage point. Total perception means to be able keep the assemblage point locked down in it new position and perceive cohesively in that new position.

These new positions were usually transformations into various other forms such as that of a coyote or a crow, for example. He taught the Nagual Julian many new positions, one of which was how to become a woman. He also taught the nagual Julian the gait of power. The death defier's interaction with Castaneda revealed the method of achieving total perception, the twin positions. If the *dreamer* fell asleep again in his *dream* in the same position that he was in when he first started *dreaming*, it enabled the *dreamer* to gain total perception in that *dreaming* in the future. Also revealed was a method of enhancing the *dreaming* attention to make it much more vivid, which is to touch the roof of the mouth with the tip of the tongue while *dreaming*.

Because don Juan did not really care for the death defier, he received only two positions, one of which was how to become a crow. Don Juan didn't like the death defier because his gifts were usually only distractions that did not enhance the search for freedom, the new seers' only goal. The death defier was one of the old seers, whose practices and indulgences were anathema to the new seers of don Juan's lineage. And his relationship with the death defier would certainly never help him to fulfill his destiny as the one nagual called on to explain the warrior's way, the search for freedom, to the outside world. The nagual Julian knew that this was to be don Juan's task and gave him extra preparation. Perhaps this is why he also had the rare opportunity to be taught by two naguals, the nagual Julian and his benefactor, the nagual Elias.

The last few years of don Juan's time on earth were very busy and taxing. He found six other apprentices that he put under his personal direction. There were five women: Lydia, Rosa, Maria Elena (La Gorda), Josefina and dona Soledad; and one man, Eligio. Don Genaro, don Juan's cohort from his party, took three male apprentices: Pablito, Benigno and

Nestor. Don Juan helped with don Genaro's apprentices and don Genaro did the same for his, including assisting with Castaneda's instruction. Also aiding with Castaneda's instruction was a nagual woman, Carol Tiggs. Don Juan found her working at a government office in Arizona and managed to secure her membership in his warrior's party without Castaneda's assistance.

The nagual woman carried books of poetry in the trunk of her car that she read aloud to don Juan. He generally only enjoyed the first one or two stanzas of a poem, feeling that the rest were usually repetitions or page fillers.

As the end of his time on earth neared, don Juan began to observe the world around him more closely, as if to memorize every detail. Castaneda described his behavior on their final trip together: "In Oaxaca, don Juan spent hours looking at mundane, trivial things, the faded color of walls, the shape of distant mountains, the pattern on cracked cement, the faces of people. Then we went to the square and sat on his favorite bench..."

Don Juan knew that although he would be able to observe the items of this world from the Third Attention, he could never again experience them with his full bodily awareness, the sensual pleasure of the beautiful and the commonplace. The immense comfort that we find in our daily world, our ordinary awareness - the position of the assemblage point taught to us by our parents - would soon be only a memory. But it would be a memory that could be kept for thousands, perhaps millions of years.

His last moments in this world were described thusly: "And then there was only a line of exquisite lights in the sky. Something like a wind seemed to make the cluster of lights contract and wriggle. There was a massive glow on one end of the line of lights where don Juan was. I thought of the plumed serpent of the Toltec legend. And then the lights were gone."

21. A Summary of Practical Applications of the Warrior's Way
(Brief discussions of how the concepts of the Warrior's Way could possibly aid and enhance solutions to problems and situations encountered in the course of everyday life. They should not be interpreted as an attempt to practice medicine or psychiatry, as the author is not a licensed professional in either field.)

"What a strange feeling: to realize that everything we think, everything we say depends on the position of the assemblage point." (8,4,109)

"...the position of the assemblage point dictates how we behave and how we feel." (7,12,200)

The discovery of the existence of the assemblage point is the most revolutionary event in human history. Because its position on the luminous energy shell determines all thoughts, feelings, physical wellness and mental health, learning to control its position is the most valuable skill that any person can ever be taught.

The position of a child's assemblage point varies wildly until, by methods that we do not understand, parents are able to help it to stabilize in a position similar to that of their own assemblage points. After this, having sufficient energy and a varied internal dialogue maintains this position, which is essential for the child's participation in the culture into which it is born.

The internal dialogue is what keeps the assemblage point fixed to its original position. (7,8,137)

A fluid and varied internal dialogue is essential because that a repetitive one begins, over time, to have the same effect that a mantra has on those who practice transcendental meditation. Thoughts are repeated to the point of becoming meaningless and the internal dialogue effectively disappears, resulting in the movement of the assemblage point. Whereas the person who meditates maintains a level of control over this movement of the assemblage point, those with repetitive internal dialogues often lose their ability to retain control and become mentally ill.

The position of the assemblage point of a person with mental illness fluctuates wildly like that of a child's or has drifted into a new position that does not allow effective interaction with others, requiring the amount of attention and persistence that a parent would lavish upon a child. This is an effort that can be provided to very few of those who are seriously mentally disturbed. The usual method of treatment is to give the patient a stable environment (like a parent would provide for a child) and to administer psychoactive drugs that move the assemblage point or at least seem to stabilize it. But since the methods of administering these drugs result in constantly varying levels of medication in the patient's system, the position of the assemblage point varies constantly also. This hinders any attempt to truly stabilize the assemblage point's position and restore the patient's ability to interact productively with others.

Having control over the internal dialogue, the ability to stop it and restart it at will, is the key to helping the millions of people who suffer from insomnia. Stopping the internal dialogue stops the avalanche of thoughts that keeps the insomniac awake. Once the internal dialogue stops, the assemblage point drifts away from the position of self-concern that is its usual position for the entire human race. The insomniac, however, has a higher level of self-concern and so must do consciously what those without insomnia do naturally. Insomniacs without the ability to stop their internal dialogue can resort to other methods to move their assemblage point away from the position of self-concern. One method is to roll the eyes in a circular motion (either clockwise or counter-clockwise). This will move the assemblage point away from its position temporarily, effectively stopping the internal dialogue. With concentration and will, the new position can be maintained long enough for sleep to occur. Another method is to try to remember and immerse oneself in the memory of pleasant dreams that one has had in the past. Since dreams occur when the assemblage point has reached a different position during sleep, immersing oneself in those memories moves the assemblage point back to that position and sleep is achieved. Another method for men is to focus the attention on the area of the body just at the tip of the sternum. Women should concentrate their attention on the womb.

"The new seers recommend a very simple act when impatience, or despair, or anger, or sadness comes their way. They recommend that warriors roll their eyes. Any direction will do; I prefer to roll mine clockwise. The movement of the eyes makes the assemblage point shift momentarily. In that movement you will find relief. This is in lieu of true mastery of *intent*." (7,16,258)

Rolling the eyes can be used as a method to alleviate conditions of extreme stress and fear. Another method is to concentrate on the exact midpoint of the body. To find the location of this center of energy, the body should be measured down to a hundredth of an inch.

Stress is also often caused by unpleasant memories from the past. Recapitulation removes much of the power to trouble us that these memories have. It takes the sting out of them, so to speak. They become more of a flat tableau rather than a living landscape.

Some of the most common sources of stress are the bad habits and behaviors that so many of us indulge in. It is recommended that we view these behaviors as a series of actions that end with an undesirable result. If any one of these actions is removed from the chain of events, the behavior is prevented. Bad habits are like a house of cards. If one card is removed the entire structure falls.

We either love or hate those who are reflections of ourselves.
(8,2,48)

For me personally this quote from *The Power of Silence* is

one of the most profound and revelatory statements about human behavior ever uttered. Our relations with other people are one of the most common causes of stress and those who bother us the most can cause extreme upset. To realize that the characteristics that annoy us to distraction in others are the characteristics that we most abhor within ourselves is vital to controlling and moderating our interaction with others. The negative side of this principle is the common phrase, "It takes one to know one." Don Juan recommended that we view those who bother us as "petty tyrants," and that we use the interactions that we have with them as a way to practice detachment and self control. He even recommended that we seek them out if none are at hand! He believed that nothing else can temper the spirit like successfully dealing with petty tyrants, which prepares a warrior to face much greater challenges.

"To act in anger, without control and discipline, to have no forbearance, is to be defeated." (7,1,43)

But it's every bit as important to know that we often love or idealize others based on characteristics that we value in ourselves. To love someone because that they share our attitudes or values comes very close to worshiping oneself, and that self-importance is never a good idea. And it can blind us to the negative side of others that can result in disastrous consequences. Those who wish to use us to their own advantage very often pretend to share our feelings and ideals. It is the classic technique of the con artist.

This philosophy applies not only to other people, but also to ideas or alternate lifestyles. Good examples of this are gay bashers, many of whom are actually secretly gay themselves; those who claim to hate hippies but actually embrace hippie ideals; those who say they hate people whose political views oppose their own. The list could go on and on. Strong feelings indicate fascination and attraction. The opposite of love is not hate, it is indifference. Don Juan stunned Castaneda when he said that those seemingly most active in helping others actually couldn't care less about them and that those seeming to do the least actually cared the most.

As noted earlier, every person is born with a different level of energy. Over time, as our energy level lessens, we become more and more susceptible to disease. But we do not become sick because that we have been exposed to germs. We are constantly exposed to germs and other environmental toxins, but we become sick because that our energy level has eroded to such an extent that we can no longer fight off the deleterious effects of these agents. Stress, self-importance, sexual activity, boredom and bad habits deplete our energy. If we address these factors before they have a chance to deplete our energy we can live a healthy life. The most beneficial aspect of a hospital stay is that we are removed from the environment in which these factors reduced our energy, giving us time to recoup our energy losses. Any medical professional can tell you that one of the most important factors in a patient's recovery is belief - belief in the power of the medications administered and belief in the knowledge and expertise of the doctor and hospital staff. Such belief reassures the patient and reduces stress and worry immensely. But the patient's separation from the environment in which they became ill is actually the most important factor of all. Poisonous personalities and situations kill by draining the energy of their "victims" who choose to remain around or in them. Illness is only a symptom of the actual problem.

Pushing disease out of the body: "... she has to push the disease away with her left hand. She must push her arm out in front of her with her hand clenched as if she were holding a knob. She must push on and on as she says out, out, out. ... she must dedicate every second of her remaining life to performing that movement." (5,2,106-107)

Pushing disease or an unwelcome feeling out of the body: He [Don Juan] made me lie down and took my right arm and bent it at my elbow. Then he turned my hand until the palm was facing the front; he curved my fingers so my hand looked as if

I were holding a doorknob, and then he began to move my arm back and forth with a circular motion that resembled the act of pushing and pulling a lever attached to a wheel. The idea was to push and pull an imaginary opposing force until one felt a heavy object, a solid body, stopping the free movements of the hand. If the hand becomes cold, stop the exercise immediately. (3,15,231-232)

Don Juan recommended that a warrior should never carry anything is his hands while walking for more that a short distance. It distorts and unbalances the body. A backpack, carrying net or shoulder bag should be used instead. And one should always stretch the entire body after any sustained period of work, sleep, sitting or walking for the same reason. He also suggested that specific methods of sleeping lead to more complete and restorative rest. One should sleep sitting up in a comfortable chair after being afraid or distressed. And taking naps while lying on the stomach with the face turned to the left and the feet hanging over the edge of the bed accomplishes the same goal. To stay warm one places a pillow over the shoulders, not touching the neck, while wearing heavy socks or keeping the shoes on.

For an energy boost, a warrior should briefly let light from any light-generating source (the most powerful being the sun) into the eyes in a careful, prescribed manner. With the eyes half closed the head is moved slowly from side to side with particular emphasis on letting light into the left eye. If you see spots, stop immediately and be careful not to let that recur in the future.

Don Juan indicated in *A Separate Reality* that he believed that the cause of meanness in adults can be tied to humiliation as a child. This should give pause to parents and caregivers who use humiliation as a form of punishment. At some point in the future they may find themselves in the hands of those they have humiliated, and the result may be unpleasant, painful or even deadly.

22. The Moment of Revelation

When we first come to the Warrior's Way we are bewildered but excited by the new possibilities it affords us until we realize that we have always been master manipulators of perception but did not know it. By holding our assemblage point in place in order to perceive this world in a sustained manner we accomplish what is actually an amazing feat of magic. And we are all *seeing* energy as it flows in the universe every moment of our waking lives, but the fixation of our assemblage point in its usual spot on the luminous shell is so powerful that we don't even know it. The Warrior's Way is only reminding us of what we already sense; that we are all masters of awareness capable of astounding feats of perception.

Exploring the possibilities of expanded perception–that the Warrior's Way has merely reminded us of–will teach us new standards of social interaction. When millions realize that being able to explore perception means drastically simplifying their lives, social friction will lessen dramatically. Pressure on the environment will lessen also.

Great times are coming! The most exciting of our history so far! Those who seek total freedom of perception find it means freedom from all needs and desires. To discover that you need nothing but your will and energy is a true moment of revelation. So that puts you at the ideal place to be at this turning point in human history!

The ultimate accomplishment of a warrior is joy. (6,4,89)

Author's Notes

The direct quotes of Juan Matus (Don Juan) most effectively illuminate and explain The Warrior's Way, as reported in the books of Carlos Castaneda. Indirect quotations are used only when necessary, and only those prefaced by, "Don Juan said that..." or "Don Juan explained that..." etc. The quotations from Don Juan's teachers and those from the other members of his warrior's party are clearly labeled as such. Each quotation is accompanied by the book, chapter and page number from which it is taken (Book, Chapter, Page Number). Both *The Teachings of Don Juan* and *A Separate Reality* have numbered chapters which are not enumerated in the index but which have been used here to make finding the relevant quote easier across the many editions of these two books that have been published through the years. For *Magical Passes* the chapter enumeration is as follows:

        Introduction
1. Magical Passes
2. Tensegrity
3. The First Series
4. The Second Series
5. The Third Series
6. The Fourth Series
7. The Fifth Series
8. The Sixth Series

Page numbers are taken from the hardcover editions since they are the most widely available versions in public and institutional libraries. The 30th anniversary edition of the first book (with Castaneda's 1998 commentary section) has been used since it will replace the original version over time.

Insertions included by the author for the sake of clarity and brevity are marked by [brackets].

    Book 1 - *The Teachings of Don Juan: A Yaqui Way Of Knowledge*
    Book 2 - *A Separate Reality*
    Book 3 - *Journey to Ixtlan*

Book 4 - *Tales of Power*
Book 5 - *The Second Ring of Power*
Book 6 - *The Eagle's Gift*
Book 7 - *The Fire From Within*
Book 8 - *The Power of Silence*
Book 9 - *The Art of Dreaming*
Book 10 - *Magical Passes*
Book 11 - *The Wheel of Time*
Book 12 - *The Active Side of Infinity*

All of Carlos Castaneda's books are available at the official website cleargreen.com and at finer booksellers worldwide.

A Note on Terminology

I have changed all instances of the use of the word "sorcerer" in quotations or paraphrases from Castaneda's reportage to the word "warrior" except when it refers to the seers of the ancient past. The term sorcerer implies the pursuit of unwarranted influence or power over others that has nothing whatsoever to do with the actions or attitudes of the new seers, modern warriors. "Sorcery" accurately describes the activities and attitudes of the old seers, but for modern usage it is archaic, sensationalistic and misleading. Some might argue that the term "warrior" is equally unfortunate as it implies a propensity for violent and destructive acts. But since warriors are not engaged in violence or destructive acts - while at the same time battling the boundaries of their personal perception in a fight to extend them as far as possible - I believe the term to be appropriate.

Why I Wrote *The End of History*

I became a student of the Warrior's Way in 1975 when I read *A Separate Reality*. Only the first four books in the series were available at that time. As noted earlier, Castaneda himself did not begin to understand the goals and requirements of the Warrior's Way until the publication of

The Eagle's Gift (the sixth book) in 1981 and the final three were not published until 1998, the year of his death. I pondered over *The Eagle's Gift*, *The Fire From Within* and particularly *The Power of Silence* for years before realizing the vast significance for the human race of the possibility of reaching the Third Attention. And it took me almost as long to accept that the discipline required by the Warrior's Way was the only way to make any real progress. If I had known at age 21 what I know now my progress would have been greatly accelerated. The energy of youth overcomes almost any obstacle it encounters.

So, *The End of History* is for the young: they still have the energy to make the changes in lifestyle required by the Warrior's Way. They are truly mankind's last and only hope against the darkness that threatens to destroy us all. Only they have a chance to prevent the horrific pain and suffering to come which, if it occurs, will dwarf even the most catastrophic events in all of human history.

But–and I cannot emphasize this enough–*The End of History* is only a condensed version of the concepts comprising the Warrior's Way. The reader will need to use the Source Notes to study in greater detail the topics and procedures discussed in Castaneda's original texts. The words of don Juan Matus (and the warriors of his party) are all that count; and only the original twelve books contain them in their entirety.

However condensed it might be, *The End of History* is the Warrior's Way undiluted. I have accepted no compromise that might make the Warrior's Way seem less difficult or dangerous than it is. Only the best of you will have the strength and courage to walk the warrior's path. You are the new leaders of all mankind and this is your time!

Appendix I

A Brief Reader's Guide to Carlos Castaneda's Books

Summary

Through the course of writing all his books on the Warrior's Way, Castaneda made an extraordinary journey from total ignorance of the Warrior's Way to an understanding of it that he expressed in a dry, academic manner. His confusion and don Juan Matus' teaching method led to the first several books being merely an introduction of the warrior's world. By the publication of *The Eagle's Gift*, Castaneda had started to realize his place, his membership in that world and began relating events in light of that new awareness. But, to me personally, the beauty, power and knowledge of the Warrior's Way are contained in the words of don Juan Matus and his party of warriors, and their words only. One must know all the books to know their words, and the Warrior's Way.

1. *The Teachings of Don Juan : A Yaqui Way of Knowledge* (1968)

An introduction to the mood and world of a warrior. Since Castaneda, a "sophisticated" university student, had no use for abstract discussions or verbal explanations of the Warrior's Way, don Juan was required to hook and maintain his interest through demonstrations of ancient practices of the seers of don Juan's tradition. The reader will note that these rituals and practices are so tightly controlled as to be considered clinical. The Structural Analysis at the end is a waste of paper. Ignore it. Castaneda's "new" commentary for the 30th anniversary edition is a good overview of the Warrior's Way, but seems designed to convince academics, not the general public, of the value of the knowledge contained in the Warrior's Way.

2. *A Separate Reality : Further Conversations with Don Juan* (1971)

More demonstrations of ancient practices and a further step into the world of the warrior.

3. *Journey to Ixtlan : The Lessons of Don Juan* (1972)
Castaneda's first breakthrough. He realizes that The Warrior's Way is a way of life and details the methods that a warrior uses to interact with people and the natural world.

4. *Tales of Power* (1974)
A very confused Castaneda tells the story of his final initiation into the warrior's world. Don Juan's other apprentices begin to play a major role. They are only slightly less confused than Castaneda, so I personally tend to take their words with a grain of salt, unless they are directly quoting don Juan or one of the other members of his party, not only in this book, but in the later ones also.

5. *The Second Ring of Power* (1977)
The confusion and anxiety of Castaneda and the other apprentices reaches its height.

6. *The Eagle's Gift* (1981)
With the help of another apprentice, Mr. Castaneda finally begins to put the pieces together enough to understand a warrior's ultimate goal : To accept the Eagle's gift - to reach the Third Attention–to escape death for as long as the Earth itself shall live.

7. *The Fire From Within* (1984)
A re-examination of some of the examples of ancient practices as they relate to Castaneda's new grasp of The Warrior's Way. Another step forward.

8. *The Power of Silence : Further Lessons Of Don Juan* (1987)
My personal favorite of all. A mysterious journey into the unknown, as don Juan Matus convinces Castaneda of the necessity of having an abstract purpose, something beyond merely himself.

9. *The Art of Dreaming* (1994)

A complete recapitulation of techniques needed to control and manipulate dreaming and a cursory overview of The Warrior's Way. A fascinating book that reveals perceptual possibilities that even don Juan was not acquainted with, courtesy of the death defier.

10. *Magical Passes* (1998)

Details a low-impact exercise program designed to tone the body and redistribute the body's energy. The pictures and diagrams in the book can be rather indefinite, so videos were produced and are available from cleargreen.com. The beginning of Castaneda's move into academic-speak.

11. *The Wheel of Time* (1998)

A compilation of quotes and concepts that attempt to guide the attitude, the mood of the warrior.

12. *The Active Side of Infinity* (1998)

A fairly complete overview of the basic concepts of the Warrior's Way in the form of a recapitulation of formative events in Castaneda's life. Castaneda's over-sophisticated analysis often obscures as well as enlightens.

Appendix II

Carlos Castaneda: Three-Pronged Nagual?

During much of the preparation for *The End of History* I firmly believed that Castaneda had been fooled into thinking he was an apprentice nagual when his actual role was that of a journalist. His apprenticeship was so entirely different from that of the rest of don Juan's apprentices (and don Juan's own apprenticeship) that I assumed he had been chosen merely to document the Warrior's Way. I thought it too much of a coincidence that don Juan's apprentice nagual happened to be a student at UCLA–with its connections to the University of California Press–in one of the biggest media centers in the world, Los Angeles. Castaneda also happened to be a graduate student in the Department of Anthropology and as so was perfectly placed to write a book with some degree of credibility. The rather convoluted tale of how don Juan and his cohorts eventually discovered Castaneda's actual energy configuration to be that of a three-pronged nagual added to my doubts. At one point I even posted on the internet an early version of Chapter 8, "The Authenticity of Castaneda's Reportage", with this assumption built in.

But in the end I decided that the wiser course was to suspend judgement. The mechanics of how the words of don Juan reached us are of minimal importance as compared to the revolutionary world view they present.

However, in the interest of full disclosure I have decided to include the deleted portions of Ch. 8 and also a list of reasons that made me come to that conclusion.

Deleted section of Ch. 8 - The Authenticity of Castaneda's Reportage

Don Juan, during his apprenticeship as a warrior, had been assigned the task of explaining the Warrior's Way to the outside world. And I do not believe that it is too much of a reach to surmise that he knew that the person who was used to transmit that information could not remain in the warrior's milieu exclusively, as is required of an apprentice. So the person he chose to use could not be a true apprentice, but had to be an outsider who would always remain an outsider. Maria Elena (La Gorda, one of don Juan's other apprentices) said to Castaneda, "He was saving you for something that's not clear yet. He kept you away from every one of us [the other apprentices] deliberately." Don Juan had to concoct an elaborate tale (that he had mistaken Castaneda for a true nagual when in actuality Castaneda was a "three-pronged nagual") to explain to him the reason he was unsuitable as a nagual for the other apprentices and Castaneda swallowed it hook, line and sinker.

Even if don Juan's seeing had been so mistaken as to make him believe that Castaneda was the new nagual, Silvio Manuel, the real power behind the throne, would never have been so fooled.

The entire course of events was foreseen by those who trained don Juan. It was no accident that Castaneda's first book emerged at the perfect time in the society best equipped to broadcast that knowledge to the entire world. And don Juan played his role impeccably. He may have had a personal hope that Castaneda would become a true warrior, but had to accept reality as it unfolded, even if it meant that Castaneda ended up being used and eventually discarded. Perhaps Castaneda sensed this on some level and that subconscious frustration powered his sexually obsessed lifestyle.

In the final analysis don Juan ended up using and exploiting Castaneda in a most ruthless fashion. It was don Juan who first suggested that Castaneda write a book when Castaneda considered that possibility to be a "joke." Don Juan later reinforced the idea by telling him to make it a magical exercise by visualizing the text in dreaming. He also encouraged Castaneda to think of him as a sorcerer, rather than as a seer. Those claiming to be seers are a dime a dozen, but a real live sorcerer; now that was a sensational find.

Castaneda was a very dumb fellow in possession of a huge megaphone. And don Juan needed that megaphone to broadcast the Warrior's Way to a large audience. Castaneda's companion at his first meeting with don Juan at the bus station in Arizona, Bill, was well known among the local Indians. Because Bill was making a sort of farewell tour of friends and places he had previously visited—and was giving away gifts—he would have been an object of local conversation. The identity and occupation of Bill's traveling companion would have been part of that conversation. After that the only task for don Juan would have been to meet Castaneda to size him up, to see if he was suitable. He knew Castaneda's personality from the moment they met - that Carlos would report his every word and deed faithfully because 1) Castaneda feared don Juan more than death and 2) Castaneda would need a steady stream of new material in order to keep the famous author gravy train going. Castaneda was taken just far enough into the world of warriors to be convinced, to say that he'd been there. But don Juan knew that Castaneda was too self-indulgent to accumulate the personal power to ever be a threat to anyone, as someone with Carlos' personality could have been if he had the power of a true nagual (a teacher of warriors). On his own, Castaneda was totally hopeless as a warrior. He was only capable of a warrior's feats (moving his assemblage point) in the presence of don Juan, one of the members of don Juan's party of warriors, or the other real apprentices of Carlos' generation. He could only act in the warrior's world when under the influence of a real warrior, which he never was.

Don Juan warned Castaneda, in a surreptitious manner, that this could be his fate during a discussion that ostensibly concerned don Juan's method of teaching. He indicated that his method required someone to dislodge the assemblage point of the apprentice from its usual position, enabling its movement. The task of the apprentice from that point was to accumulate the necessary energy to dislodge the assemblage point themselves, a task at which Castaneda failed. Castaneda's two apprentices Taisha Abelar and Florinda Donner-Grau, who were given a limited amount of training by don Juan, might have been able at the beginning of their association to help him move his assemblage point. But once that Castaneda drew them into his web of sexual and psychological intrigue, their energy was sapped in the same way that Castaneda's was. "He [don Juan] told me that your [Castaneda's] spirit takes prisoners," was what Dona Soledad (another of don Juan's apprentices) said to Castaneda at one point. Don Juan was right.

Carlos Castaneda: Apprentice Nagual or Journalist?

1) He was kept away from the other apprentices except in very limited circumstances, the opposite of don Juan's training as a nagual. Don Juan even warned the other apprentices to stay away from him, saying that Castaneda would enslave them and that his spirit took prisoners.
2) His "training" was irregular and episodic, again the opposite of don Juan's, but what would be expected to be given to a dilettante/journalist.
3) The *seeing* of both don Juan and his more powerful cohort Silvio Manuel would have to have been mistaken for Castaneda to be considered an apprentice nagual.
4) That portion of the "rule" that pertains to naguals, The Rule Of The Nagual, contains nothing about the possibility of a three-pronged nagual, which is what Castaneda was eventually told was the reason for his unsuitability for dealing with the other apprentices. Castaneda did, however, write in *The Eagle's Gift* that the nagual woman revealed that part of the rule that applied to a three-pronged nagual just before she departed for the Third Attention with the rest of don Juan's party, but Castaneda did not reveal it in any of his writings. I've wondered if Eligio, don Juan's most talented apprentice, was meant to be the actual new nagual (Castaneda was told that Eligio's role in the new nagual's party was that of courier). But Eligio was so gifted that he was ready to leave the world with don Juan's party, stranding the other actual apprentices in this world without a nagual to lead them. So they were unavoidably left behind to enter the Third Attention singly or in small groups if they were able. And the fact that Eligio, even after leaving the world, was trying to guide the other

apprentices - communicating with them through their dreaming - seems to support my contention. Don Juan did try to take the apprentices into the Third Attention once, as the Nagual Julian had tried unsuccessfully to do with don Juan's own party, but they were not ready. And don Juan had told Pablito that he had a chance to become the nagual someday.

5) Florinda, from don Juan's party, was left behind on the fringes of the Third Attention to "instruct" Castaneda and the other apprentices on the art of *stalking*, but was more likely there to ensure that he did not attempt to control or influence the others to follow his destructive lifestyle. She succeeded in this goal except for Maria Elena, Carol Tiggs, Taisha Abelar and Florinda Donner-Grau.

6) Castaneda played no part in securing "his" nagual woman, Carol Tiggs. Again, this is the opposite of don Juan's role in securing Olinda, don Juan's nagual woman.

7) Don Juan did begin engaging other apprentices after he found Castaneda, but that does not mean that they were meant to be for a warrior's party with Castaneda as nagual. They were likely intended to be part of a group that was truly meant to continue don Juan's line. Don Juan's destiny was to explain the Warrior's Way to the outside world and any other task may have been put on hold until he had begun to fulfill that destiny.

8) Castaneda was given two female apprentices as a "three-pronged nagual" either because they came into don Juan's world too late for proper training or because they were found to be totally unsuited to such training. And there is the possibility that don Juan hoped that they would someday be strong enough to divert Castaneda from his disastrous lifestyle, a lifestyle that eventually began to bring discredit to the Warrior's Way itself.

9) Castaneda was never able to move his assemblage point of his own volition. Except for a couple of instances of involuntary movement of his assemblage point, he required the presence of an actual warrior to help him dislodge it. He never had the high energy (which is the definitive feature of a true nagual) required to do so. This was undoubtedly don Juan's

fail-safe mechanism to ensure that Castaneda, with his grossly indulgent personality, could not act on his own.

10) Castaneda never gained control of the two inorganic beings (allies) that he inherited once don Juan's party had left the world. Only a warrior with the true detachment and high energy could have done so, and Castaneda had neither.

The following statement may be callous and cruel but is nevertheless true: Castaneda's fate doesn't matter. Whether he was meant to be a true nagual, a three-pronged nagual or a dilettante/observer is not important. He certainly deserves credit and praise for taking the risks he did during his interactions with don Juan. He did succeed in bringing the Warrior's Way to the world's attention and that is all that matters.

Appendix III

The Return of the Nagual Woman

The return of the nagual woman, Carol Tiggs, after leaving the world with don Juan and his party, is one of the most controversial aspects of Castaneda's post-apprenticeship history. To understand this surprising development we need first to discuss some of the events that occurred previously.

Don Juan and the old seer known as the death defier did not get along. Don Juan resented being forced to deal with him and the death defier undoubtedly resented don Juan's attitude and the fact that he had no choice but to be a freeloader, a burden on all the naguals of don Juan's lineage. To survive, he had to have energy that he could only obtain from the naguals of don Juan's line. He needed a permanent solution. Being one of the ruthless and self-indulgent old seers, he concocted a plan that he hoped would accomplish this goal and also give him the perverse satisfaction of derailing don Juan's transition to the Third Attention.

Using the mastery of awareness he had cultivated for thousands of years, he intended in the Second Attention a dream world for himself that was an exact replica of a small town in ancient Mexico where he and other old seers had lived. To intend this dream world forward–to hold it in place and maintain it as a viable destination with himself as an inhabitant–he needed much more energy than he alone could provide. To obtain this energy he extracted a large amount from Castaneda during their encounter that occurred (as described in *The Art Of Dreaming*) not long before don Juan and his party were due to leave for the Third Attention.

But his real masterstroke was merging his awareness with that of the nagual woman, Carol Tiggs, prior to meeting with Castaneda. He ruthlessly exploited Carol Tiggs' inexperience and naivety to literally hijack both her awareness and her energy. The nagual woman had such tremendous energy that the death defier hoped, with their combined resources, they could re-route don Juan's entire party to the death defier's dream world and thereby hold it in place—intend it forward—indefinitely. Once they arrived at this alternate destination he would only have to use his mastery of the old sorcerer's techniques to fixate the awareness of the entire group—to freeze the position of their assemblage points—and make the perception of that world the only possible one. The death defier did not seek the total freedom of the Third Attention. He sought the freedom to indulge his eccentricities and desire for power. What better place to do that than an entirely new world where he controlled all he surveyed?

But somewhere in its execution, the death defier's plan failed. The nagual woman's return to this world indicates that he had at least been able to take *her* into his dream world in the Second Attention. If he was able to take any of the other members of don Juan's party there (and keep them there) is not known. We do know that Carol Tiggs eventually escaped the death defier's dream world and returned to this one a broken woman, her energy sapped. She eventually became a mere pawn in Castaneda's group of followers, a shadow of her former self.

We also know that don Juan and don Genaro did reach the Third Attention since they used the ability—which only inorganic beings have—to project their images back into this world. They did this together once and don Juan did it by himself another time. And don Juan's most powerful apprentice, Eligio, who managed to attach himself to don Juan's party and leave the world with them, communicated with two of don Juan's apprentices (Josefina and Maria Elena) through *dreaming*. This would not have been possible if his awareness had been fixated by the death defier.

Castaneda and his group were shocked to the core by the nagual woman's return and—dimly apprehending what had occurred—began to wonder if don Juan and his entire party were stuck in the Second Attention. But they were too busy with their pursuit of idle pleasures to give the matter much consideration and swept up the nagual woman into their egomaniacal obsessions. When don Juan made his second, solo appearance in this world (in the lobby of a San Francisco hotel in 1991) both Florinda Donner-Grau and Carol Tiggs walked right by him as if he didn't exist. Carol Tiggs later claimed that she had no memory of the entire chain of events after merging with the death defier, so she was unable (or unwilling) to enlighten the others as to what had happened–if they had even cared to know.

What has become apparent, on further consideration, is that don Juan knew something was up and that his entire enterprise could be threatened by the death defier's merger of his awareness with the nagual woman's. He knew enough to tell Carol Tiggs to stash some money in a few hidden places in Tucson, Arizona, where she found herself after returning. If he knew enough to foresee this development, he undoubtedly had enough forewarning to attempt to thwart the death defier's plan. If he had the energy to do so completely, and assure the safety of his entire party (except for the nagual woman), is not known.

An interesting foreshadowing of the nagual woman's fate is to be found in *The Eagle's Gift*. When Castaneda and Maria Elena are first retrieving their memories of the nagual woman from the dream world of heightened awareness, Maria Elena declares that the nagual woman is "shipwrecked" and that they should try to find her. Castaneda then corrects Maria Elena, telling her that the nagual woman was no longer in this world. But he was not really sure of anything at that point.

Richard Jennings (a.k.a. Corey Donovan), a former member of Castaneda's inner circle, has done searches of public records that seem to indicate Carol Tiggs had actually returned several years before she resumed contact with Castaneda in 1985. The embarrassment and humiliation she must have felt over her failure to fulfill her role as the nagual woman and what amounted to a total betrayal of don Juan's trust would certainly explain her reluctance to see Castaneda and his group. Her story of having been gone for the ten years before she re-established contact with Castaneda (and having no memory of that time period) would have been quite useful for the purpose of protecting her from any consequence that could have resulted had Castaneda and his group known the actual chain of events. Jennings was unable to turn up any instance of Carol Tiggs' appearance on the public record between 1972, when she changed her name to Elizabeth Austin, and 1980, when she graduated from California Acupuncture College. He surmised that she first enrolled there in the fall of 1977, although it could have been as early as fall 1976. According to Castaneda, the nagual woman left with don Juan's party in 1973. So she may have been gone for as long as four years before her actual return.

Her activities upon her return appear to be consistent with what any young woman might do after undergoing a shattering, life-changing experience. She tried to get on with her life by enrolling in school and getting married. Her marriage, however, did not last and she was divorced in 1984, not long before she resumed contact with Castaneda. Amy Wallace (Castaneda's on-again-off-again companion for several years and the author of a book, *Sorcerer's Apprentice*, which documents her experiences with Castaneda and his group) claimed that Carol Tiggs never left in the first place. But she had no direct knowledge to support this claim except for Carol Tiggs' sometimes contradictory statements. At one point Wallace says that the nagual woman "openly admitted to having lived an ordinary life," but provides no details and no direct quotes to support this. Carol Tiggs did attempt to live an "ordinary life" during the years immediately following her return, but for Wallace to draw such a definitive conclusion from the statements of such an over-stressed and psychologically tortured individual certainly amounts to questionable and rather careless journalism. She probably extrapolated this assumption from Richard Jennings' research, which was available when she wrote her book.

Wallace was a witness, however, to Carol Tiggs' seeming obsession with "betrayers" and being betrayed. She devoted a separate chapter in *Sorcerer's Apprentice* to the nagual woman's oft-repeated tirades on this topic; most of which would end with Carol Tiggs saying, "I should know, I'm a betrayer too." Her betrayal of don Juan and his warriors led her to project these feelings onto others.

Wallace believed that Carol Tiggs had merely fallen from favor with Castaneda and that was why she left the group for over ten years. But if that was so then why was her return greeted with such fanfare by Castaneda and his inner circle? The return of a woman whom Wallace referred to as a "near-mediocrity" would hardly justify the mythologizing that resulted. And her public prominence (and major financial participation) within Castaneda's group after her return would not have been conferred upon just another paramour/groupie.

Unfortunately, despite its value in exposing the bizarre and poisonous reality of Castaneda's last few years, *Sorcerer's Apprentice* is filled with errors and inaccuracies large and small that mark it as a textbook example of sloppy journalism:
1) Ch. 1, Pg. 7: Wallace says that in *A Separate Reality* Castaneda "met beings from other worlds, which he called *inorganics* (her italics)." In fact, Castaneda only referred to inorganic beings as "allies" in *A Separate Reality*. The term "inorganic beings" was not introduced to describe the allies until the publication of *The Fire From Within*, from which point they were always referred to as inorganic beings, never "inorganics".
2) Ch. 1, Pg. 8: Wallace refers to anyone entering the Third Attention "retaining one's body", when a merely cursory reading of Castaneda's work makes it quite clear that the opposite is true.
3) Ch. 1, Pg 8: Wallace confuses the Second Attention with the Third Attention; saying that when one burns from within they reach the Second Attention when she should have said the Third Attention. Then in the next sentence she mentions the Third Attention as if it were somehow separate from the level of awareness one reaches after "burning from within".
4) Ch. 1, Pgs. 8-9: Wallace implies that Castaneda led his readers to believe that he had the power to read minds at will when he made no such statement. He did say that don Juan had this ability.
5) Ch. 1, Pg. 9: Wallace implies that Castaneda led his readers to believe that he had the ability to "shapeshift" at will when in fact he said no such thing. He described incidents where he did

indeed change his form, but these occurred only when he was under the influence of don Juan or the female seer known as "La Catalina".

6) Ch. 1, Pg. 9: Wallace describes Castaneda's interactions with don Juan's other apprentices resulting in "Castaneda breaking ties with his wards", when in fact they had been informed that he was not a suitable leader for them and so *they* broke ties with *him*.

7) Ch. 1, Pg. 13: Wallace says that reaching inner silence was referred to by don Juan as *seeing* when in fact no such equivalence was ever stated or implied. Don Juan was never so careless as to say that the first *step* to *seeing*, reaching inner silence, was equivalent to reaching that level of awareness. Perhaps she was confused when she read Silvio Manuel's incantation for times when a warrior feels his task is greater than his abilities. It reads, in part, "I have no thoughts, so I will *see*." But Silvio Manuel's words of encouragement are meant to be a condensed, shorthand version of a phenomenon that requires other intermediate steps before the goal of *seeing* is reached. Immediately after giving Castaneda the incantation, Silvio Manuel demonstrated the technique of *seeing* human beings as luminous eggs. Castaneda was already deep in heightened awareness, a stable, fixated *dreaming position*, at this point. Silvio Manuel showed him how to focus his eyes briefly on the point of the second attention while engaging intent, and Castaneda *saw*.

8) Ch. 2, Pg. 33: Wallace misquotes Castaneda when describing the incident from *A Separate Reality* when don Juan's son Eulalio was killed. Wallace says don Juan "shifted his awareness, moved his assemblage point". However, the concept of the assemblage point was not introduced into Castaneda's writings until *The Fire From Within*.

9) Ch. 6, Pg. 57: Wallace says that she does not remember Juan Tuma from Castaneda's books, but he was twice mentioned prominently in *The Eagle's Gift* and listed (as *John* Tuma - an anglicized spelling - but pretty clear nonetheless) as a member of don Juan's party in the Foreword to *The Fire From Within*. In his second mention in *The Eagle's Gift* it is revealed that it

was at Juan Tuma's home where Castaneda first had peyote, but Castaneda referred to him in *The Teachings of Don Juan* only as John.

10) Ch. 7, Pg. 66: Wallace states that the death defier and Carol Tiggs rescued the blue scout from the inorganic beings' world after they had merged when in fact it was the merging of the blue scout's energy with that of Castaneda's which allowed her to escape the inorganic beings' world. Carol Tiggs, don Juan and other members of his party rescued *Castaneda* from the inorganic beings' world, but this was prior to Carol Tiggs merging with the death defier, according to the sequence of events described in *The Art of Dreaming*.

11) Ch. 12, Pg. 100: Wallace says that recapitulation was "barely explained in his books" by Castaneda, when it was actually described in minute detail by Florinda (a warrior from don Juan's own party) in *The Eagle's Gift*. It was again described in detail in *The Active Side of Infinity* and its importance was at least mentioned in every book after *The Eagle's Gift* except for *The Fire From Within*.

12) Ch. 14, Pg. 119: Wallace again confuses the Second Attention with the Third Attention when she says that expulsion from Castaneda's group would mean "losing heaven." The Second Attention contains a world that resembles the traditional descriptions of heaven, but what Wallace means to say is that expulsion would mean losing the chance for total freedom—entering the Third Attention.

13) Ch. 15, Pg. 135: Wallace says that Castaneda had written about being a short-order cook in Arizona in his books when it was actually mentioned only in Florinda Donner's book, *Being-In-Dreaming*.

14) Ch. 25, Pg. 213: Wallace says that Castaneda "wrote" that don Juan had cured him of his cigarette addiction with long walks in the desert while "pretending to be lost." There is no such incident (or any such incidents) in any of Castaneda's books. He related this event in an interview with Graciela Corvalan that appeared in *Magical Blend* magazine (#14) in 1985.

15) Ch. 35, Pg. 303: Wallace states that the nagual Julian had

"erotically mesmerized a woman who was to become his apprentice," when in fact the woman she is referring to, Talia, became the nagual Elias' apprentice and then became a member of the nagual Julian's warrior party—not his apprentice.

16) Appendix A, Pg. 409: Wallace states that Mark Silliphant was the son of Sterling Silliphant, when he was actually his brother.

This list shows that Amy Wallace' many careless and totally unnecessary inaccuracies—combined with her emotional involvement with the subjects of her book—cast serious doubt on her objectivity and ability to draw credible conclusions as sweeping as her assertion that Carol Tiggs' never left this world at all, but was actually living with her mother and her husband the entire time that she was supposed to be in the Second Attention.

Appendix IV

The Blue Scout

Another controversial aspect of Castaneda's post-apprenticeship life was the Blue Scout. The original Blue Scout made her first (and only) appearance in *The Art Of Dreaming* as an individual who was the prisoner of the inorganic beings. The Blue Scout appeared to Castaneda in the form of a young girl. Was this her actual, original configuration or was it one that he/she assumed for the purpose of attracting Castaneda's sympathy and concern? There is nothing quite as heart wrenching as a helpless little girl and whoever this being actually was hoped that impression would be enough to secure Castaneda's assistance. I personally think that he/she was a being like the death defier who could take on almost any form he/she chose to assume at any given moment. But the Blue Scout was obviously never a flesh-and-blood little girl. Young girls do not appear out of thin air or float in and out of rooms like ghosts. After being freed from the inorganic beings, she hung around long enough to say her thanks and then went on her way.

As for the mortal Blue Scout who was a member of Castaneda's group in his post-apprenticeship years, according to research done by Richard Jennings (a.k.a. Corey Donovan) she was a woman originally named Patty Partin who met Castaneda in the 1970's and became one of his most important acolytes. Her title, the Blue Scout, was obviously an honorarium bestowed on her for her important contribution to Castaneda's increasingly bizarre way of life. She was his hatchet-person, so to speak, taking on the unpleasant task of weeding out those who had fallen from Castaneda's favor. Castaneda bestowed many honorary titles on his followers over the years: Orange Scout, Chacmools, Energy Trackers, etc., and this is how the quite mortal Patty Partin came to be the Blue Scout. In order to secure her authority and status among Castaneda's followers, a back story was created for her that, as has been reported, became quite convoluted as time passed.

Why Castaneda indulged in this endeavor can only be explained by his dictatorial role as nagual to his group. His power corrupted him, then killed him. Don Juan had warned him that having sex could lead to his downfall, that he could lose his mind, but Castaneda did not listen. His ever-escalating megalomania affected the other members of the group too, until they began to tell wild tales that they assumed that others would accept blindly.

I do think, however, that Castaneda retained enough mental acuity to separate his indulgences in his personal playground from what he actually put into his books. The books were his task given to him by men infinitely more powerful than he ever was, and as it turned out, ever could be. He feared don Juan and Silvio Manuel more than death itself; and he feared that even from the Third Attention, they could reach out and crush him like a bug any time they decided to do so. With that in mind, I believe that the actual flesh and blood people Castaneda mentioned in his work (Florinda Donner-Grau, Taisha Abelar and Carol Tiggs) were what he portrayed them to be. As they stated in their own books, Florinda Donner-Grau and Taisha Abelar spent very little time with don Juan. They came into his orbit too late for sufficient training to accompany him to the Third Attention and so had to be left behind. As is also apparent from their books, they were both extremely self-indulgent and did not have the wisdom to separate themselves from Castaneda, as don Juan's other apprentices all (except Maria Elena) did. Carol Tiggs, having been sidetracked by the death defier from her role as the nagual woman, ended up stuck with Castaneda also.

Maria Elena's mistake of remaining attached to Castaneda's group turned out to be fatal. Having grown disgusted with Castaneda and his group's behavior, she prepared to enter the Third Attention. But at the last second she tried to take Florinda Donner-Grau with her by force. Donner-Grau's resistance drained Maria Elena's energy at this crucial moment and she died before their (Donner-Grau, Abelar, Castaneda) eyes. Florinda, the female seer from don Juan's party who had remained behind to help finish training

Florinda Donner-Grau, Taisha Abelar and Castaneda himself, made no such mistake. She departed for the Third Attention, but not before denouncing them as self-important idiots.

It was no coincidence that Castaneda died not long after finishing his last substantial work, *The Active Side of Infinity*. His task was complete and the spirit had no further use for him. His presence from that point on was only an obstacle to the fulfillment of the spirit's intent.

All in all, a very sad ending for such a promising beginning. But what's worse is the effect on the public's perception of the Warrior's Way itself. Castaneda and his group's conduct has added much fuel for the fires of skepticism.

Nevertheless, the words of don Juan remain. Their power and truth will eventually overcome all doubts and mankind will move on to the next stage in our evolution, the Third Attention.

Appendix V

Debunking De Mille

In the following section, I will debunk the debunker. The writings of Richard de Mille have been purported to prove that Castaneda's books are works of fiction. I will show de Mille's claims to be gross over-simplifications and exaggerations by examining his two books–*Castaneda's Journey* and *The Don Juan Papers*–and his appearance in the movie *Carlos Castaneda: Enigma of a Sorcerer.* I will not attempt to address every accusation and insinuation from all this material. That would require a separate book of its own and would be a waste of both mine and the reader's time. I will, however, address the major allegations.

Castaneda's Journey

"But I thought: If I were a struggling graduate student or an obscure professor, and some guy came along and wrote four best sellers in a row while I was trying to finish my dissertation or get some puny five-page paper published in the *American Anthropologist*, I might have some snide and unfair things to say about him, too."

Richard de Mille

Castaneda's Journey

In Ch. 3, 'Fact Or Fiction', de Mille claims that, "Carlos first heard about *seeing* six years after he first *saw*." He refers to a brief reference to *seeing* by don Juan that occurred on Jan. 29, 1962 and alleges that this incident, by predating another brief conversation that Castaneda and don Juan had about *seeing* on May 21, 1968, shows Castaneda's work to be fictional.

In the context of the events of Jan. 29, 1962 that were reported in *Journey To Ixtlan*, don Juan's very brief reference to *seeing* would have been interpreted by Castaneda at this early stage of his apprenticeship as only a vague allusion to a psychic phenomena comparable to how a psychic "sees" into the future. In the conversation of May 21, 1968 reported in *A Separate Reality*, it was unmistakable that don Juan was referring to a different way of perceiving the world quite separate from the (at that time) imprecise references to *seeing* in 1962. But because *Journey to Ixtlan* was published after *A Separate Reality*, Castaneda was able to appropriately italicize and highlight this brief mention of *seeing*, having the experiences of 1968-1972 to guide him in his writing of *Journey to Ixtlan*. If de Mille was paying a little more attention, he would have used as an example the conversation between don Juan and Castaneda that occurred sometime before May 14, 1962. This interchange, reported by Castaneda in the Introduction to *A Separate Reality*, came much closer to actually illuminating what *seeing* was all about. But since don Juan was still being very elusive about the topic (he talked about it as a way of knowing, which again could have been interpreted as an allusion to an ambiguous psychic phenomenon, and said, "...unless you understand the ways of a man who knows, it is impossible to talk about...*seeing*.") Castaneda still did not catch on to what don Juan truly meant by *seeing*.

Also in Chapter 3, de Mille asserts that sewing the eyelids and mouth of a lizard shut using a choya thorn as a needle and a fiber from an agave as a thread would be impossible because the thickness of both the choya thorn needle and the agave fiber would have split the lizard's tissues apart so that they could not be sealed. Declaring this "...delicate task he [Castaneda] had never practiced before nor seen demonstrated" to be impossible, de Mille asserts that this incident must be fictional.

But again, by negligence or convenience, de Mille is not paying proper attention to what Castaneda actually wrote.

The directions given by don Juan for sewing the mouth of one lizard and the eyelids of a second lizard require a *wooden* needle for the actual sewing, fibers of agave and one thorn of a choya. The details of the actual sequence of their usage is not described by don Juan in Castaneda's account. The fiber of a *dried* agave is thin enough to be attached to a wooden needle. The sharp end of the choya thorn would be used to make round holes in the lizard's tissues through which the wooden needle and agave fiber could pass without tearing and splitting the eyelids and mouth, thus sealing them together. It would have been a difficult task, which is exactly how Castaneda described it, but he had seen the two lizards that don Juan had used when he demonstrated the ritual and so had an previous example to follow.

The next section of "Fact Or Fiction" deals with the distinguished ethno-botanist R. Gordon Wasson's concerns about Castaneda's work as expressed in the reviews of the first four books he wrote for *Economic Botany*. Having expressed these concerns in a letter to Castaneda, he wrote in his review of *Journey To Ixtlan* that, "He replied fully and intelligently (garbled by de Mille to "...fully and frankly..."), and then I met him in New York and later in California. He was obviously an honest and serious young man, and *I have no reason to change my mind about him now* [my italics]." Wasson goes on to discuss the twelve pages of xeroxed, re-copied field notes that Castaneda submitted for his inspection, and apart from a minor concern about some of the dates being different from those listed for the events in *Journey to Ixtlan*—which Wasson himself explains away—relates no other qualms about their veracity or accuracy of translation.

But Wasson's satisfaction with Castaneda's willingness to document his field work means nothing to de Mille. With no basis whatsoever except supposed inconsistencies in the Spanish-English translations (and an unreasoning suspicion) he writes, "Subject to refutation by long-awaited proofs from Castaneda, it is my solemn conviction that those 12 pages did not exist before Wasson wrote his letter, that they were manufactured for the occasion, and that they are the only pages of Spanish field notes to come out of Carlos's dozen years in the desert." De Mille posits Wasson as an expert (which he was) and then rejects Wasson's opinion.

And that is not the only example of de Mille's readiness to distort the views of this expert to suit his own agenda. Earlier in this chapter, de Mille states that Wasson's opinion of Castaneda's work was that Castaneda had become, "a poor pilgrim lost on his way to his own Ixtlan." The complete quote from Wasson's review of *Journey to Ixtlan* is as follows:

"But Castaneda vacillates between targets. Instead of offering us a romance, he bids for the respectful attention of anthropologists and ethnologists. He also strives to supply the publisher with what is needed to sell the book. Castaneda is himself a poor pilgrim lost on his way to his own Ixtlan."

Wasson is clearly referring to how Castaneda portrays himself in *Journey To Ixtlan* as someone to whom a mass audience could easily relate, not expressing an evaluation of Castaneda's diligence or veracity. After using and abusing Wasson's words to suit his own purpose, it is surprising that de Mille was able to solicit a quote from Wasson for the jacket of *Castaneda's Journey*. Was "My word! You have done your homework well" another partial quotation designed to distort Wasson's real meaning? Was it actually followed by "...but your willingness to distort my views as well as Castaneda's work is unacceptable"? Or perhaps Wasson had become intimidated by de Mille and hoped to head off a similarly unanswerable inquisition into his own work by appearing to praise de Mille's book. Walter Goldschmidt, who wrote the foreword to *The Teachings of Don Juan*, certainly felt that de Mille was trying to intimidate those he contacted concerning Castaneda. After de Mille sent him a letter that de Mille himself admits was "...far from ingratiating," Goldschmidt filed a formal complaint with the Committee on Scientific and Professional Ethics and Conduct of the American Psychological Association that accused de Mille of attempting "intellectual blackmail."

Over time, Goldschmidt did indeed become cowed by the shrill chorus of media and academic criticism based almost exclusively on de Mille's flimsy accusations. In a *Los Angeles Times* interview published Nov. 20, 2005, he was asked if he regretted writing the foreword to *The Teachings of Don Juan* and replied, "Yes, I'm a little ashamed of it, but not that much. If you read what I wrote you will see that I was not all that complimentary. What I assumed was that he had taken peyote and he was recording those experiences as if they really happened. In that sense, I thought it was true. My first paragraph reads, in part--'this book is both ethnography and allegory.'" The reader will note that Goldschmidt makes no definitive statement concerning Castaneda's veracity; he effectively sidesteps the question so that he can get on with promoting his latest book (and his life).

Chapter 4, "What Happened At UCLA?", is based only on de Mille's allegation that Castaneda's work is fictional. But de Mille offers no proof of any lapse in judgment or any misconduct by any of UCLA's faculty. If anything, he offers up proof of the authenticity of Castaneda's work by stating that five faculty members signed their names to Castaneda's doctoral dissertation and by reprinting the quote from one faculty member used in the Time magazine cover story in 1973. That quote: "...his truth as a witness is not in question," seems definitive to me.

Chapter 5, "A Man Of Novels," was de Mille's first attempt at the "Alleglossary" he included in his second book on Castaneda, *The Don Juan Papers* and has the same flavor. Any quote or concept that can be dredged from the fields of anthropology, psychology, ancient mysticism, etc., that uses even one word found in Castaneda's books is claimed as one of the sources Castaneda plagiarized to produce his "fiction." Only one example has enough similarity to fit de Mille's program, the description of the human body when seen as pure energy that William Walker Atkinson derived from ancient Eastern mystics. Considering that both the warriors of don Juan's lineage and the Eastern mystics were seeing the same thing–the body perceived as pure energy–how markedly could they differ? Similar descriptions of the same phenomena are not a confirmation of plagiarism on Castaneda's part, but an affirmation that seers throughout the ages have been plowing the same field, the various positions that the assemblage point can assume. These various positions have led to remarkably consistent descriptions of heaven, hell, "God" and many other common perceptions by seers of the past.

Chapter 6, "Trickster Teacher", takes page after page of mean-spirited drivel to get to one comparison of anthropologist Peter Furst's account of a Huichol shaman named Ramon Medina Silva's demonstration of balance at a waterfall to Castaneda's account of don Genaro Flores at a waterfall demonstrating the energy fibers produced by the body called *will* in an attempt to trigger *seeing* in Castaneda and two of don Juan's other apprentices. Aside from the similarity in setting and the fact that both men took off their sandals before proceeding, the two incidents have no other similarities significant enough to conclusively demonstrate that Castaneda borrowed Furst's account for insertion into *A Separate Reality*.

Looking at the two events in the glancing, superficial fashion that de Mille specializes in might yield strong parallels. But when one considers the differing intents of the demonstrators and the fact that Silva was leaping from rock to rock on large stones (balancing on one leg while under the influence of alcohol) that were clearly visible to his observers while don Genaro was using rocks that could hardly be seen, the incidents each have a very different basis.

Photographs taken by Furst of Silva's demonstration of balance at a waterfall show Silva to be wearing a large, showy costume. Such an elaborate outfit would have caught the wind and caused serious balance difficulties unless the wearer was engaged in an activity little more dangerous than crossing a stream by going from stone to stone; a photo opportunity for his American visitors.

In *The Don Juan Papers*, de Mille recounts his conversations with another witness to Silva at the waterfall in 1966, anthropologist Barbara Myerhoff, who was a doctoral candidate in the UCLA Dept. of Anthropology at the time. She said that after returning from Mexico, she told Castaneda about what she had witnessed and Castaneda replied that it was "like don Genaro," even though Castaneda's account of don Genaro's waterfall demonstration was dated as occurring in 1968 in *A Separate Reality*. But Myerhoff was very unsure of the chronology of her conversation with Castaneda about Silva, so it probably did not occur until after Castaneda witnessed don Genaro's display in October 1968.

The fact that both Myerhoff and Castaneda were UCLA students in the department of Anthropology makes the possibility that Castaneda appropriated her and Furst's story for *A Separate Reality* too remote for serious consideration. Any hint of plagiarism would have been noted and would have had seriously adverse effects on Castaneda's standing in the department. No student would be so bold as to crib such a notable incident and not expect to be expelled from the department and probably the university itself. And the fact that Myerhoff (as reported by de Mille) defended her dissertation, which included the Silva demonstration, to a UCLA faculty committee in the same month that Castaneda witnessed don Genaro's certainly does not mean that Castaneda's account was fictional.

The bold craziness that it would have required for Castaneda to plagiarize Furst and Myerhoff's story is the kind of meat that gets de Mille's juices flowing most freely. The superficial similarities in the accounts and Myerhoff's vacillations concerning her conversation about it with Castaneda amount to one of de Mille's big contentions, one of his big guns in attempting to discredit Castaneda. But the fact that both Furst and Castaneda presented these accounts in a 1970 series of lectures at UCLA on an equal basis without any recrimination on Furst's part concerning any alleged borrowing signals Furst's acceptance of the validity of Castaneda's narrative. Furst later said that the stories were "strikingly similar," but he had nothing else to say on the subject. If Furst was willing to accept the validity of Castaneda's account, then how can we agree with de Mille's refusal to accept it?

While we are on this topic, let's cover de Mille's assertion in *The Don Juan Papers* that since Castaneda did not meet don Genaro until 1968, Castaneda's statement to Myerhoff that Silva's demonstration was like don Genaro's is suspect. But if Myerhoff was unsure about the chronology of events, how can de Mille be sure of them?

The remaining formal chapters of *Castaneda's Journey* contain little of interest except de Mille's refusal to accept that the warriors of don Juan's lineage might have a different conception of what the terms tonal and nagual mean as compared to what they mean to other indigenous cultures. If Castaneda uses terms that are similar to usages by other groups de Mille finds that unacceptable. If he uses concepts that differ from other groups de Mille finds that equally unacceptable.

"Carlos-One And Carlos-Two" is the first of the appendices of *Castaneda's Journey*. It begins with de Mille listing all the psychoactive plant-related events and the incidents unrelated to the usage of those plants. Then de Mille decides how that Castaneda should have written his books if he desired to convince bottom-feeders like de Mille of their authenticity. Then we arrive at another alleged discrepancy concerning the mention of *seeing*. But the same circumstances and conditions detailed above apply to this accusation also, and are made even clearer in this instance by Castaneda's comment, "I wanted to ask what I was supposed to see [no italics]..." during the Dec. 1961 event.

In "Carlos-One And Carlos-Two", de Mille makes much of Castaneda's 1965 encounter with someone who don Juan says has taken on don Juan's appearance in an effort to fool Castaneda, but whose replication of don Juan's body language and mannerisms are so obviously wrong that Castaneda believes it to be a female attempting to imitate don Juan. Discussing the incident with don Juan, Castaneda wrote, "The conversation began with speculations about the identity of a *female* person who had allegedly taken my soul." De Mille leaps on this rather innocuous detail to assert that the female person had to be the female sorcerer La Catalina and that Castaneda's failure to remember her in this instance when he had said in the early part of *A Separate Reality* that his encounter with La Catalina was still "...vivid as if it had just happened," means that the 1965 incident was merely the fictive device of a serialist author anticipating a sequel. De Mille believed that this supposed incongruity proved conclusively that either *The Teachings of Don Juan* or *Journey to Ixtlan* was fiction.

In this 1965 incident, don Juan was undoubtedly acting unlike himself in an attempt to fool Castaneda. The "female person" who Castaneda believed to be imitating don Juan maintained don Juan's appearance for the entire event, making a precise identification impossible. The possibility that La Catalina had the ability to assume don Juan's form to perfection is too remote for serious consideration. But since Castaneda did not know this, the mere suggestion that it might have been La Catalina or another unknown female sorcerer served to drive Castaneda's fear even deeper.

The speculation on the identity of the female person was also a teaching device on don Juan's part to accomplish the same goal. At this point, Castaneda—after his fearful encounters with La Catalina in 1962—did not even want to contemplate the possibility that she had returned to terrorize him again. Also, don Juan had noticed that during Castaneda's earlier encounters with La Catalina that Castaneda was very attracted to her as a woman, lessening the psychological impact of her possible return. The mention of the chance that it might be another female sorcerer was meant to increase Castaneda's uncertainty and unease over the incident. Castaneda had not been harmed by La Catalina in the past, so her effectiveness as a "worthy opponent" had lessened considerably. Once again, de Mille oversimplifies don Juan's subtle and sophisticated teaching method in an attempt to score cheap points.

This section of "Carlos-One And Carlos-Two" ends with a viciously racist parody by de Mille of how that La Catalina might have verbally threatened Castaneda if they had encountered each other face to face. Passages like this—which are spread throughout *Castaneda's Journey*—make the task of disproving de Mille's arrogant hypotheses something like swimming in sewage.

"Carlos-One And Carlos-Two" concludes with de Mille's most ridiculous accusation of the lot; that Castaneda had to "experience" all of the events chronicled in *Journey to Ixtlan*, write the book, attend classes and give lectures—all between October 1970 and the book's publication in late 1972. De Mille is so intent on attacking Castaneda's credibility that he conveniently forgets that almost all of the events discussed in *Journey to Ixtlan* (Castaneda's doctoral dissertation) had occurred years before and that doctoral candidates preparing their dissertation usually have few or no classes to attend.

Castaneda's Journey ends with de Mille's dissatisfaction with Castaneda's translations of conversations and descriptions originally rendered in Spanish that result in English rich in idiomatic and slang phrases. Castaneda's translations undoubtedly were affected by his years of interactions with native English-speaking students and faculty at both Los Angeles City College and UCLA. These supposed anomalies mean nothing more than that.

The Don Juan Papers

After the flimsy hypotheses and jeering, condescending style of *Castaneda's Journey* failed to convince anyone but those who read it (and Castaneda's books) in the most glancing and superficial way possible, de Mille coughed up *The Don Juan Papers*. In this book his hyperbole escalates to new heights of near-hysterical shrillness.

The overstatements begin in Chapter 2, "The Shaman of Academe," with the first of three alleged "proofs" that Castaneda's books are a hoax. De Mille states: "Carlos meets a certain witch named La Catalina for the first time in 1962 and *again* [de Mille's italics] for the first time in 1965." Castaneda did not know the identity of the person whom don Juan had led him to believe has assumed don Juan's form in the 1965 incident de Mille is referring to. To say that Castaneda met someone "again" when that person could not be identified is absurd.

Then de Mille moves on to say that: "Though he [Castaneda] learns a lot about *seeing* in 1962, unaccountably he has never heard of it in 1968." Don Juan had referred to *seeing* briefly in December 1961 and January 1962, but no serious discussion of the topic took place either time.

The most detailed conversation about *seeing* from 1962 was one reported by Castaneda in the Introduction to *A Separate Reality*. It occurred sometime prior to May 14, 1962, when Castaneda visited don Juan's friend Sacateca. But this conversation was still so indefinite that Castaneda had no real understanding of the concept (and don Juan indicated that Castaneda was still not ready to approach the subject). Castaneda's reaction to don Juan saying later that Sacateca had *seen* him, danced and stopped him [Castaneda] with his *will* was, "His statements sounded like gibberish to me." A man who has learned "a lot" about *seeing* would not react thusly.

Castaneda did not begin to understand what don Juan meant by seeing until their discussion on May 25, 1968, when don Juan described it in detail as a different way of perceiving that was not merely looking. De Mille is referring to their brief conversation about seeing on May 21, 1968 when he claims that Castaneda had "...never heard of it." This is an intentional oversimplification of Castaneda's reaction ("I wanted to know what he meant by that...") when don Juan said that the best time to *see* was in darkness. But this was the first time that Castaneda was able to discern a real difference between *seeing* and looking, since looking is difficult or impossible in darkness. So it was at this point Castaneda finally began to get a glimmer that *seeing* had to be a separate phenomenon from looking (or psychic intuition).

Next de Mille spits up this ludicrous exaggeration: "*The Teachings* tells a gothic tale full of fear and wonder, barren of joy and amusement." In actuality there are over a dozen examples in *The Teachings of Don Juan* of don Juan's laughter lightening the mood of various events. He mostly laughs at Castaneda's absurdities, but that is vastly different from being "...barren of joy and amusement."

Then we arrive at de Mille's "...second kind of proof," the "...absence of convincing detail and the presence of implausible detail." In this section de Mille expects the reader to believe that he is familiar with every animal species (and its peculiarities of behavior) that Castaneda and don Juan could have met in any location; that he knows the exact size of any tree that Castaneda might have climbed; that he knows the weather conditions of each day that they spent together; that he knows which locations Castaneda might have disguised to preserve don Juan's anonymity and which locations were substituted for them. And the reader will notice that the criteria he sets up conveniently enables him to reject any and all passages that do not pass his omniscient judgment. Castaneda's statement in the introduction to *Journey to Ixtlan*, "Since I was capable of writing down most of what was said in the beginning of the apprenticeship, and everything that was said in the later phases of it..." is transformed by de Mille into "With prodigious speed and skill he writes down 'everything' [de Mille's quotation marks] don Juan says to him under the most unlikely conditions." Actually, Castaneda's skills as a stenographer were considerable. A fellow student in the UCLA Dept. of Anthropology, Jose Cuellar, described his ability as, "...more than adequate. the amount of detail he was able to record is incredible, both verbal and non-verbal behavior. My question was how can you do that under normal circumstances, let alone under the influence of psychotropic drugs? It seemed impossible to me, as a first year graduate student, to take notes that fast. But he could. He demonstrated it to us. He used a steno pad and had developed his own system of shorthand."

After that rather dishonest and deceptive transmogrification of Castaneda's words, we come to a high point in de Mille's parade of delusions: "No one but Castaneda has seen don Juan." Castaneda was introduced to don Juan by his anthropologist friend Bill (tentatively identified as William Laurence Campbell, who this source called an "amateur archaeologist"; Margaret Runyan Castaneda believed him to be Alan Morrison, who, "spoke only a few words of Spanish"), who had spoken to don Juan on at least one other occasion before he and Castaneda met don Juan in Nogales, Arizona. De Mille also ignores the incident in *Tales of Power* when Castaneda and don Juan were pursued in Mexico City by one of Castaneda's friends who wanted to meet don Juan.

Next we come to de Mille's claim that, "Castaneda met serious early resistance from skeptics in the UCLA faculty." But in this chapter de Mille names only one; Ralph Beals, a man de Mille praises and derides according to his particular purpose at the moment. In the Note for this section, de Mille mentions two others who he described as "chairmen," but does not detail his conversations with them except to call them "skeptical." But de Mille doesn't say exactly what they were skeptical about. Castaneda's friend and former fellow student, Dr. Jose Cuellar, described the long and difficult process of Castaneda's dissertation being approved as being a matter of inter-departmental conflict between members of the dissertation committee. "One side said it wasn't analytical enough and the other side said it was too analytical. So basically what he did was disband his dissertation committee."

Cuellar also said that *A Separate Reality* was submitted as a dissertation but was not accepted because of the disagreements cited above. De Mille implies that questions about Castaneda's truthfulness were the cause of their skepticism when it is just as likely they were uncertain about the final form the dissertation should take. Castaneda himself confirmed this in a letter to Margaret Runyan Castaneda, saying, "The point of argument is the nature of the material...and how I have treated it."

Next, regarding Castaneda's field notes and tape recordings, de Mille states that there was no presentation of these materials that might have confirmed their existence. Unless de Mille attended every interaction Castaneda had with UCLA faculty members and his dissertation committees, that accusation is further evidence of an arrogant omniscience that attempts to present biased supposition as fact.

De Mille's accusation that there were no actual field notes was flatly contradicted by Margaret Runyan Castaneda in her book *A Magical Journey with Carlos Castaneda*. In it she writes, "Carlos's years in the field had generated several hundred pages of field notes, some photographs, a brief 16mm film and some tape-recorded interviews, most of which he later denied having. He had reworked his field notes all along, trying to put then in a more readable form."

On the subject of Castaneda's field notes, it seems obvious to me that no presentation of the field notes - raw, edited, in whatever quantity - would ever satisfy those like de Mille whose intellectual worldview is exposed as crude and primitive by the revelations of, to them, a mere Indian.

And to finish with the topics of UCLA skeptics and "alleged" field notes, let's go over Dr. Ralph Beals' uncertainty about Castaneda's field work. In his article "Sonoran Fantasy or Coming of Age", (*American Anthropologist*, June 1978), he writes, "He did not disclose his shaman's residence but implied that he had been making weekend visits to him on the Yaqui River. This seemed improbable, for it is over a thousand-mile round trip, too far to permit weekend ethnographic sessions. I pressed him to show me some of his field notes, but he became evasive and dropped from sight, not too difficult in a large department. I assumed he had dropped out of the University."

Castaneda's field trips *were* long and very disruptive to his progress as a graduate student. Barbara Myerhoff said that, "He had handfuls of incompletes. He was always disappearing and coming back." And Castaneda did actually drop out of UCLA in 1965 because of what Margaret Runyan Castaneda said were money problems, but there could have been other factors (too may Incompletes) at work also. Part of Castaneda's reason for being vague and evasive with Beals was probably Beals' interest in details that could have violated Castaneda's promise to maintain don Juan's anonymity. When Beals "pressed" him for field notes that could have revealed locations, names etc., Castaneda had no choice but to avoid providing him with these materials should every other faculty member and fellow student make the same request. As word had gotten around the department that Castaneda had found a real shaman/informant, interest had grown considerably. Would some of those faculty members and students go looking for don Juan themselves? Considering these factors, presenting the field notes and any other materials would have to be done only on a need-to-know basis. And let's not forget the de Mille hypothesis that any field notes extant had all been manufactured to fit the occasion. If that was the case, then Castaneda could easily have come up with some for Beals' inspection.

De Mille's "...third kind of proof" is any kind of similarity in wording, phrasing, concept or usage of plants that may have any relation–no matter how insignificant– to Castaneda's work. In my critique of *Castaneda's Journey*, I've already dealt the first example offered here: the similarity of William Walker Atkinson's description of the human aura to don Juan's description of the human body when *seen* as pure energy. De Mille's second example is a severely edited quotation from an article that appeared in *Psychedelic Review* magazine in 1977–"Four Psilocybin Experiences" by Frederic Swain and three other anonymous authors. De Mille's abstract is taken from the second experience (by one of the anonymous authors) and is edited by (all the italics are his) de Mille to:

"*My eyes* were closed, and a large *black* pool started to open up *in front of* them. I was able to see a *red* spot. I was aware of a most unusual *odor*, and of different parts of my body getting extremely *warm*, which felt extremely good."

The text of the complete sentences is actually:

"I sat down, put my head back and closed my eyes. B. put on [Allen] Ginsberg's *(sic)* recording. With my head back and my feet stretched out, the space for the first time changed its dimension. It flattened out. Ginsberg drifted to me across this level plain, then started to fade. My eyes were closed, and a large black pool started to open up in front of them. As the space continued to expand, a small white object seemed to be coming toward me or perhaps I was going toward it - extremely brilliant. As I came closer, I was able to see a red spot in the white. The one time during the entire session that I was aware of any taste or odor was when I came back and there seemed to be a strange taste in my mouth and a most unusual odor. I really don't know what it was or how to describe it - the first time I have come into contact with it. The plain was gone and I became aware of different parts of my body getting warm, which felt extremely good."

Then de Mille abstracts another quotation for comparison from Castaneda's first experience with datura in *The Teachings Of Don Juan*:

"What was very outstanding was the pungent *odor* of the water. It smelled like cockroaches. I got very *warm*, and blood rushed to my ears. I saw *a red spot in front of my eyes.* 'What would have happened if I had not seen red?' 'You would have seen *black*.' 'What happens to those who see red?' 'An effect of pleasure.' "

The complete sentences actually read:

"I took it automatically, and without deliberation drank all the water [containing the datura preparation]. It tasted somewhat bitter, although the bitterness was hardly noticeable. What was very outstanding was the pungent odor of the water. It smelled like cockroaches. Almost immediately I began to sweat. I got very warm, and blood rushed to my ears. I saw a red spot in front of my eyes, and the muscles of my stomach began to contract in painful cramps. After a while, even though I felt no more pain, I began to get cold and perspiration literally soaked me. Don Juan asked me if I saw blackness or black spots in front of my eyes. I told him that I was seeing everything in red. Then he asked me if I was afraid. His questions were meaningless to me. I told him that I was obviously afraid, but he asked me again if I was afraid of her. I did not understand what he meant and I said yes. He laughed and said that I was not really afraid. He asked me if I still saw red. All I was seeing was a huge red spot in front of my eyes. I felt better after a while. Gradually the nervous spasms disappeared, leaving only an aching, pleasant tiredness and an intense desire to sleep. I couldn't keep my eyes open, although I could still hear don Juan's voice. I fell asleep. But the sensation of my being submerged in a deep red persisted all night. I even had dreams in red. I woke up on Saturday about 3:00 P. M. I had slept almost two days. I found don Juan sitting in front of his house dozing. He smiled at me. 'Everything went fine the other night,' he said. 'You saw red and that's all that is important.' 'What would have happened if I had not seen red?' 'You would have seen black, and that is a bad sign.' 'What happens to those who see red?' 'They do not vomit, and the root gives them an effect of pleasure, which means they are strong and of violent nature - something that the weed likes. That is the way she entices.' "

Let's examine de Mille's analysis of these two passages:

"This goes beyond accidental correspondence. These two passages, each of which is drawn from less than a page of original text, have in common at least five specific word combinations as well as seven ideas: drug hallucination, seeing black, seeing red, unusual odor, parts of the body, getting warm, and pleasure."

First, there are only *three* word combinations that can said to be similar: "red spot", "in front of my eyes" and "unusual (pungent) odor." The anonymous artist who was experiencing psilocybin saw a red spot on a white object that appeared from a pool of black. Castaneda saw only a red spot that expanded until he was seeing everything in red. Castaneda did not see black at any time. Don Juan mentioned seeing black as a possible effect of datura use but Castaneda did not experience it. Any kind of drug-related visual hallucination would be described as being "in front of my eyes." The anonymous artist experienced an unusual odor unbidden as a side effect. Castaneda was referring to the actual smell of the datura preparation.

Of the "seven ideas" that de Mille mentions, four of them (drug hallucination, parts of the body, getting warm, pleasure) are common to almost any experience of ingesting powerful psychoactive plants. The user hallucinates. The user's heart beats faster, leading to a sensation of warmth that might be experienced subjectively in various parts of the body. And aside from the expansion of consciousness that those who take psychoactive plants seek, the overall effect is most usually one of pleasure. If the effects were extremely unpleasant, the usages of these plants would not have become a tradition handed down through the ages. The other three "ideas", when seen in context, are mere coincidence.

As we can clearly see from the above examples, de Mille is concerned solely with superficial similarities. Content, context and meaning have no relevance for him. The way de Mille edits the passages strongly implies that the content and context of both are similar when they are actually totally different. This is another example of the deceptive oversimplifications that de Mille indulges in so freely. He counts on the reader not having the original texts at hand that he claims that Castaneda is borrowing from and assumes that no one will go back and check Castaneda's actual words against those texts (or against his accusations). This methodology applies to the entirety of his writings on Castaneda, and especially to the so-called 'Alleglossary' contained in *The Don Juan Papers*.

Chapter 2 concludes with de Mille's allegation that Castaneda's account of using don Juan's smoking mixture containing psychoactive mushrooms must be fiction because, "...nobody had actually tried to smoke them until Castaneda's books were published, and then it didn't work." Once again, this is a vast oversimplification of the process of consuming the smoking mixture. The act of pulling air through the pipe caused the fine powder, the mushrooms, to be sucked into Castaneda's mouth, resulting in their ingestion orally. In the introduction to *A Separate Reality*, Castaneda described the procedure. "The process of 'smoking' consisted of ingesting the fine mushroom powder, which did not incinerate, and inhaling the smoke of the other five plants that made up the mixture." At this point , the attentive reader might wonder how that ingesting the mushroom powder orally would result in the rather immediate hallucinogenic effect. The most immediate effect, "...my whole body was numb, mentholated" would be caused by the other plants in the mixture. Because the mushroom powder - though it does not incinerate - would undoubtedly give off fumes by being in such close proximity to the burning plants in the mixture, its effects would be felt rather quickly. And it is well known that the fastest way any to get any medicine into the bloodstream when consuming it orally is to is to grind it into powder. But the amount of time that actually passes between when Castaneda begins to smoke the mixture and when he begins to feel its psychoactive effects is not specifically quantified. So accurately judging the immediacy of its effects is not possible.

As we have seen before, de Mille tries to reduce a multifaceted procedure into an activity as banal as smoking a cigarette. He also wants the reader to believe that he is aware of how that hallucinogenic mushrooms are used by every culture in the world who uses them when he says that, "...nobody had actually tried to smoke them..." And the only way to prove that smoking don Juan's mushroom mixture "...didn't work" is for de Mille to have smoked the mixture or to have witnessed someone else doing so.

One of the sources that de Mille listed as supporting his claim that that smoking mushrooms would not work was Steven Pollock's "The Psilocybin Mushroom Pandemic", an article published in *Journal of Psychedelic Drugs* in 1975. Pollock writes that, "Curious mushroom stone artifacts, usually from Guatemala but also from the Mexican states of Tabasco and Vera Cruz, have been dated between 1000 and 300 B. C. and would strongly suggest that an ancestral mushroom cult flourished in the culture of the highland Maya." This means that the indigenous peoples of Central America have been using psychoactive mushrooms for perhaps the last 3000 years. It is certainly quite likely that over 3000 years many elaborate uses and preparations had been discovered for various species of mushrooms aside from simply ingesting them orally.

Pollock concludes that section of his piece by noting that those who smoked mushrooms in Popayan experienced effects of shorter duration than what would be achieved by eating them. He says that, "I later gave the smoking method a trial but received only a headache." He doesn't say if he used the same mixture that those in Popayan were using, what method he actually used to smoke mushrooms or what species of mushroom he did smoke. This is science? It is, actually, since science has been used by Euro-centric cultures to dominate the rest of the world since its inception. Belittling the customs of "primitive" cultures (and "primitives" like don Juan) has given the Western powers an excuse to "civilize" them and to exterminate their native religious and shamanic traditions.

Another issue unaddressed by de Mille or Pollock is the elaborate nature of Castaneda's "literary device." Would a hoaxer allegedly too lazy to do any actual fieldwork bother to invent such an elaborate method of consuming psychoactive mushrooms when he could simply create an story that would have fit more closely with the accounts of others that de Mille claims Castaneda plagiarized so freely? As noted earlier, Castaneda's critics want to have it both ways. Anything new is fiction. Anything remotely similar to other traditions or practices is plagiarized.

Chapter 6, "Validity Is Not Authenticity", showcases de Mille's twisted, convoluted logic and culminates in a claim that is so outrageous it defies belief. To say that don Juan and Castaneda stalked rabbits bare-handed–when they actually used traps assembled from materials found in the immediate environment– demonstrates again that de Mille is counting on his readers being unfamiliar with Castaneda's work to such an extent that any accusation, no matter how extreme, is acceptable to him. How much more evidence do we need to prove that this man was willing to stoop to any level necessary to discredit Castaneda?

After Chapter 6, de Mille's wild accusations are repeated endlessly in the remaining chapters, as if saying something often enough will make it so. Then we reach the crown jewel of his folly: the "Alleglossary." Any word, phrase, idea or concept that can possibly be construed to be similar–no matter how remote the fashion–is taken to be plagiarism on Castaneda's part from any literature in any field previous to, contemporaneous with, or even published after, Castaneda's books. But the totally unique concepts that Castaneda wrote about in his books from *The Eagle's Gift* forward are not addressed, even though de Mille had access to all twelve of Castaneda's books by the time that the final revised version of *The Don Juan Papers* was published in 2000. There are no entries for: Assemblage Point, Inorganic Beings ("Ally" is listed as being comparable to an account of Tibetan sorcerers wrestling with re-animated corpses !?!), First Attention, Second Attention, Third Attention, Energy Body, Intent,

Recapitulation, The Rule Of The Nagual, The Death Defier(s), Flyers, The Eagle, The Eagle's Commands, Commanding Intent, Emanations, Alternate Worlds, Self-Importance, Internal Dialogue, Inner Silence, The Right Way Of Walking, Conserving Sexual Energy, Redistributing Energy, Silent Knowledge, Scouts, The Dreaming Emissary, The Voice Of *Seeing*, The Human Mold, Impeccability, Detachment, The Earth's Boost, and many others.

So almost all of the most important ideas and concepts of the Warrior's Way have no precedent that de Mille could be bothered to conjure up. There are entries for *Dreaming*, *Seeing* and *Stalking*, but they are so farcical as to be unworthy of consideration by anyone who has read Castaneda's books attentively.

De Mille's Appearance in *Carlos Castaneda: Enigma of a Sorcerer*

Interviewed in Ralph Torjan's movie *Carlos Castaneda: Enigma of a Sorcerer*, de Mille asserts that there are "three kinds of evidence" in Castaneda's books to prove that they are fictional. The first is the "internal inconsistency of don Juan's character" and "many other internal inconsistencies."

The alleged inconsistencies in don Juan's character represent Castaneda's changing focus regarding the proper presentation of his work. The first book, *The Teachings of Don Juan*, was meant to be a "serious" academic treatise, so don Juan's jokes and frequent laughter were de-emphasized as being somewhat inappropriate to such an undertaking. The second half of Castaneda's apprenticeship, which began with *A Separate Reality*, was marked by a lighter mood which made the inclusion in the text of moments of levity appropriate - as they were part of the teaching method. *Journey to Ixtlan* continued this mode of description and included the earlier moments of jokes and laughter that had been occurring all along, but did not fit the more "academic" mood of *The Teachings of Don Juan*. As I noted earlier, don Juan frequently used laughter to lighten the atmosphere in *The Teachings of*

Don Juan, but its overall tone was more serious than the rest of Castaneda's books.

The language and eloquence with which don Juan expressed his thoughts, however, was very consistent until Castaneda's last few books. Don Juan's more professorial tone in the later books reflects Castaneda's preoccupation with establishing the academic legitimacy he had long been denied.

Don Juan was educated by the nagual Julian's female apprentices; some of whom came from the same well-educated background from which the nagual Julian himself emerged. The household's wealth gave them access to any extant literature they desired. Don Juan's love of reading and frequent travels throughout Mexico and the southwestern United States resulted in a most articulate personality, leaving the only "inconsistencies" to how Castaneda chose to translate his words. It is ironic that de Mille should accuse Castaneda of putting the words of other writers into don Juan's mouth when writers don Juan himself read may have influenced how he articulated the concepts of the Warrior's Way as he taught them to Castaneda.

Don Juan spent a significant amount of his life in Arizona. He undoubtedly interacted with many people who spoke English in the sixty-nine years before he met Castaneda. To assume that a man of his intelligence did not absorb or occasionally use English slang phrases as interjections or exclamations would be to ignore his background totally. Castaneda may have modified some of his translations to make them more contemporaneous, but to assume that don Juan knew no English is either meant to be an attack on his intellectual capacity or a facile excuse for criticizing Castaneda's work.

Castaneda and don Juan met at a Greyhound bus terminal in Nogales, Arizona, where at least a passing familiarity with English would be most helpful, if not vital, to navigating the ins and outs of bus travel. In the decades before bi-lingual signage became a common feature of American life, knowing at least some English was crucial to anyone traveling in the southwestern United States. And don Juan, being born in

Arizona, was an American citizen who had undoubtedly visited various government offices in the course of his life and carried papers or identification issued by them. Dealing with the questions of government bureaucrats would also have required some knowledge of English.

Once again, as we can see, de Mille attempts to oversimplify a complicated set of circumstances to score cheap points.

The other so-called "internal inconsistencies" that de Mille does not actually discuss in *Enigma of a Sorcerer* I have dealt with in my critiques of *Castaneda's Journey* and *The Don Juan Papers*.

De Mille's second kind of "evidence" was the "Inconsistency of Castaneda's desert and the desert that has been observed by people who actually went to the desert."

Castaneda's promise to preserve don Juan's anonymity was not limited to the use of pseudonyms for him and the other members of his party. It also required that the locations where events actually happened be obscured. This has been totally ignored by Castaneda's detractors, resulting in specious comments regarding inappropriate weather conditions and inaccurate descriptions about events that perhaps did not even occur in the very general geographic descriptions Castaneda provided.

De Mille's third kind of "evidence" is "Two hundred examples of echoes from the literature of... written by other people, about all the things that Castaneda is writing about. The language of other people comes out of don Juan's mouth."

Any well-read speaker or writer's phraseology is often subconsciously influenced by other writers, particularly if they are relating phenomena closely allied to another author's subject area. Here de Mille has softened what he previously implied was Castaneda's outright plagiarism to "echoes from the literature." I have dealt with the "two hundred examples" in my previous critique of the "Alleglossary" contained in *The Don Juan Papers*.

Summary

The seers of don Juan's lineage were a previously undiscovered group until Castaneda began writing about them. As a separate entity, they had their own unique expressive concepts and usages of psychoactive plants. But because they were describing the human milieu, some similarities exist in the methods and descriptions they used to express their participation in the act of being alive. The sophisticated subtleties of don Juan's life, his teaching method, and his way of expressing himself can't be reduced to simple yes or no, all or nothing banalities that de Mille and other critics insist are the only way of determining their "truth". Their "truth" was determined in advance and the "facts" made to fit their "truth." De Mille's willingness to use any device, no matter how deceptive or illogical, to attack Castaneda is part of a larger battle that is often referred to as the Culture Wars. Any expression of spirituality, alternate view of reality, or philosophy that could threaten the existing social order is to be obliterated by any means necessary. The social status and livelihood of people like de Mille depends on it. The slowly dawning realization that the West's official religion, its official belief system, Science, is no more an accurate description of reality than many others, will be fought ruthlessly.

Big changes cause even bigger reactions from those unwilling to be a part of those changes. They will attack with any tool at their command, no matter how vile. De Mille was one of their previous champions. There will be others.

Contemporaneous Witnesses

There were several individuals who knew Castaneda during the years of his apprenticeship and these witnesses reported that he informed them of his interactions with don Juan as they were occurring.

Margaret Runyan Castaneda:
1) "One day in the summer of 1960 Carlos told me he had met a man he wanted to study with and it would mean being away

for days or weeks at a time." [Then she was asked, "Did he mention the man's name?"] "Don Juan."

2) "He [don Juan] was a real Indian. Somebody Carlos actually was making trips to see."

Dr. C. Scott Littleton:

1) "Yes, I'm convinced that there was indeed a prototype of don Juan & that he probably was a Yaqui who moved rather freely between the Tucson area and northern Sonora. I also recall Carlos telling me that he never saw the guy again, at least in the flesh, after he, Nestor and Pablito jumped off the Ixtlan cliff at the climax of their initiation. He also said that his mentor died shortly thereafter." [Castaneda had a habit of referring to entering into the Third Attention as an alternate way of dying.]

2) "I have no reason whatsoever to suspect a hoax. I have known [Castaneda] too long and too well to doubt his professional integrity."

3) "What's my overall assessment of Castaneda? First of all, he was definitely not--I repeat NOT!--a hoaxer. Do I accept everything he said at its face value? No, but then, at bottom, neither did he, even though it faithfully reflected his perceived experiences with Don Juan, Don Genaro, and the rest. What he was trying to do was record a shamanic world-view & to play the game, as it were, by Don Juan's rules. He also was convinced that sorcery was "problematic," that is, that it was more than cultural nonsense, as most anthropologists had painted it up to that time. It's this aspect, I think, together with the implicitly racist idea that no "Chicano" (which, of course, he wasn't) could possibly write as well as he did in English, that triggered the attempts by Richard De Mille, et al., to 'expose' him as a fraud. But they never succeeded."

Dr. Jose Cuellar:
Q: In your day to day contact with him, did you see the development of his ideas?

Cuellar: I think that was an experience that all of us in the department had - Carlos was the kind of person who would naturally share his ideas. He would corner you someplace or come running in and say, "Hey, guess what happened? I was with Don Juan and this happened. What do you think?" Or he would corner a faculty member and say, "I was just going through my notes and look what I've discovered." He was constantly doing that.

Q: Any particular examples come to mind?

Cuellar: There are a number. One I remember was where Genaro and Don Juan hid his car. I was in the UCLA library with a couple of other students and faculty members, and Carlos came running in and began to relate the incident in a very animated fashion. Incidentally, he discussed the incident in the context of having someone else with him at the time, an Anglo male, I believe, but later on in the text I think it turns out to be just him.

Q: So you could see the consistency between the experiences in Mexico and what later came out in the books?

Cuellar: Yes. The ethnographic incidents that he reports in the book he also related on a personal level...at different points in time as he collected the data and came back and was analyzing the information. Another one was when Don Juan told him how to deal with a child that was unmanageable. And the *coyote* incident...when he was talking to a bilingual *coyote*. He told us about that around the time it happened. And there were others. [Ellipses and italics included in the original text]

Q: That's a question a lot of people are asking. *Did* this stuff really happen? It seems to me there is no simple answer to that question. Can we really differentiate between the experience and the interpretation?

Cuellar: Right. But I guess one question is, did the ethnographic incidents happen the way he reports them. And the answer to that seems to be, from my experience and the kind of contact that I had with him, *yes*, those incidents did happen. And I say that because he reported them over a long period of time. [Italics from original text]

Q: Did Castaneda ever, in talking to you, give any indication

other than what's in the books, of what or who Don Juan is?
Cuellar: No. Basically the descriptions he gave me are consistent with what has emerged in the books.

Dr. Ralph Beals: "The beginnings of Castaneda's interest in the Yaqui have some bearing on the problem of intent or understanding. Early in his career at the University of California, Los Angeles, Castaneda asked me whether, in view of the works about the Yaqui published by Edward Spicer (1940, 1954) and myself (Beals 1943, 1945), I thought further useful study among them was possible. He was interested in them partly because he could visit them on his own limited resources. Later he spoke enthusiastically about his visit to the Yaqui River and soon came to tell me about his contact with a Yaqui shaman. He asked if I thought it justifiable to concentrate on him as an informant rather than to develop some more conventional ethnographic problem. As neither Spicer nor I had encountered anything resembling true shamanism, I approved the idea. After all, in such a complex and somewhat closed culture as that of the Yaqui, Spicer and I could well have failed to uncover shamanistic practices. Castaneda later spoke vaguely but enthusiastically about his contacts. He did not disclose the shaman's residence but implied that he had been making weekend visits to him on the Yaqui River....Other critics have doubted Don Juan's very existence. In light of my earlier contacts with Castaneda given previously, I personally believe that someone called Don Juan by Castaneda exists."

Dr. Barbara Myerhoff: "There may very well have been, in the beginning, an experience with a concrete person. Otherwise, why would Carlos have said to me, 'Come down. Meet him. Come with me'? I'm still not convinced he was completely lying to me, all the time. Even the waterfall episode was not just Carlos reflecting back to me. There was something besides. Somehow from my experiences of fieldwork I get a feeling he is building on an exchange with another person. I'm not ready to give that up. He told me lots of things I subsequently read in his books. He was always disappearing [from graduate school] and coming back."

Dr. Clement Meighan (Speaking to the Editorial Board of the University of California Press before the publication of *The Teachings of Don Juan*): "I can believe what he's telling me. It was the same thing he'd been telling everybody for months. The sort of things he is coming in with are too damn good. Even to fake it, you'd have to study anthropology for ten years in order to provide the kind of convincers or data he comes up with. I've known him since he was an undergraduate student here and I'm absolutely convinced that he is an extremely creative thinker, that he's doing anthropology. He's working in an area of cognitive learning and the whole cross-cultural thing. He's put his finger on things that no other anthropologist has even been able to get at, partly by luck and partly because of his particular personality. He's able to get information that other anthropologists can't get because he looks like an Indian and speaks Spanish fluently and because he's a smart listener."

Michael Harner: "While it was flattering to be referred to as a 'genuine researcher' whose work is a source of Carlos Castaneda's data by Robert Bly in his review of 'The Second Ring of Power' (Jan. 22), I must lodge a protest in the interest of accuracy and fairness to Castaneda and his readers. Mr. Bly makes the mistake, as do others, such as Richard de Mille in 'Castaneda's Journey,' who are not really knowledgeable about shamanism, of assuming that similarities between Castaneda's material and that published by others is due to plagiarism by Castaneda. They apparently are unaware that remarkable parallels exist in shamanic belief and practice throughout the primitive world. I am thoroughly conversant with Castaneda's publications; I have known him for a decade and a half; and *I am not familiar with any evidence that he has borrowed material from my works* [my italics]. It is unfortunate that the persons chosen to review Castaneda's books are not really experts on shamanism. Whatever Castaneda's faults, he is one of the very few Westerners who have ever been able to communicate the nature of the shamanic experience. In this sense he conveys a deep truth, although his specific details can often be justifiably questioned. Who is the more significant conveyer of truth, Castaneda or a plodding ethnographer who gets [garbled] second-hand details right, but who never has had a shamanic experience and misses the spirit of shamanism?

Finally, the current attacks on Castaneda often smack of ethnocentrism. I could hardly believe my eyes (speaking of a separate reality) when Bly rejected the possibility that we could help our own personal development by learning from 'cultures more primitive than ours' and preached instead, 'only by reaching to the work of a more highly articulated culture can your interior energy come forth.' Christian missionaries have been saying more or less the same thing in the Upper Amazon jungle for decades. The Indians there still don't believe it, and neither do I. What elitist Victorian hogwash!"

[In *The Don Juan Papers*, de Mille jumps on "...although his specific details can often be justifiably questioned" to assert that these questions discredit Castaneda's work. But from my reading of his statement, Harner seems to be saying that he is curious about why certain procedures were performed the way they were; how these procedures came into existence; and other questions that an anthropologist might have about the nuts and bolts of Castaneda's work. The statement, to me, seems to say that Harner would have liked to "talk shop" with Castaneda in an effort to better understand, not to discredit.]

Source Notes

Introduction

"composed of energy" (9,1,3)
"body is perceived as pure energy" (8,Introduction,15-16)
"bright spot on the luminous shell" (8,Introduction,15-16)
"position can be altered" (8,4,164-165)
"changing the content" (8,3,76-77)
"determine our moods" (7,12,200)
"600 positions" (12,12,180)(10,5,118)
"merge it with the universe" (7,7,120)
"as long as the Earth itself lasts" (12,13,192)
"great dome" (5,4,211-213)
"usual mode of living" (10,Introduction,3)
"conserve sufficient energy" (7,9,150)(7,4,69-71)
(7,1,29)(8,4,123)(8,6,248-249)(10,Introduction,2-4)

Chapter 1 - The Spirit

"immeasurable collection of energy fields" (8,Introduction,15-16)
"Eagle's emanations" (8,Introduction,15-16)
"the force that powers the Eagle's emanations" (8,Introduction,12)
"intent, the abstract, the Spirit" (8,1,31)
"gifts of the Spirit" (7,15,237)
"clean her connecting link" (8,6,247)
"her command becomes the Spirit's command" (7,7,125)(7,16,257)
"Impeccable men and women do not need a teacher" (7,11,178)
"the known, the unknown and the unknowable" (7,3,55)
"assemblage point accesses the unknown" (7,3,46-47)
"A warrior trusts his personal power" (3,14,204)
"Instead of focusing energy on the Spirit" (6,1,27)
"The only thing we can possess" (3,14,202)
"no way to pray to the Spirit" (6,13,177)

"The Spirit can only assist the warrior" (12,Introduction,10)
"the inevitability of that acquiescence" (10,Introduction,7)
(12,3,72)

Chapter 2 - The Third Attention

"all people who choose to do so" (7,1,18-19)
"sustainable for an almost infinite duration" (7,7,120)
"the Third Attention is the ultimate, final evolution" (10,5,104)
"the fire from within" (7,11,183)
"the enhancement of awareness" (7,3,50-51)
"collects and assimilates the awareness" (7,3,50-51)
"phenomenon that we have no real way of understanding" (7,3,53)
"Our awareness will be food for the Eagle eventually" (10,5,104)
"We can choose to be happy or to be miserable" (5,5,271)(3,15,221)
"assemblage point locked in its usual position" (12,7,106 &108)
"Words have magical power" (8,3,101)
"drilled into us through constant repetition" (9,2,34)
"the somersault of thought into the inconceivable" (8,4,133)

Chapter 3 - Conserving Energy

"Human beings are born with a finite supply of energy" (10,Introduction,3)(10,1,14-15)
"The human activity that uses up most of our energy" (7,2,29)
"The internal dialogue also keeps our assemblage points fixed " (7,8,137)
"the right way of walking" (4,1,21)(4,12,232)
"A warrior accumulates inner silence" (12,7,103-108)(10,5,128)
"a dot of pomegranate red emerges" (12,12,174)
"conserve our sexual energy" (7,4,69&71)
"Death taps us when we run out of energy" (3,12,167)
"where one finds the most beautiful" (6,14,273-274)
"a warrior sees opportunity, and grabs it" (3,18,278)
"expelling foreign energy filaments" (6,14,289-292)

"recapitulation is a substitute" (9,8,149)(12,10,148)(10,5,102-103)
"an event called the usher" (12,11,148-149)
"The number and variety of magical passes" (10,2,24)
"which most would call intuition" (8,1,34)
"the voice of *seeing*" (7,4,66-67)
"To trigger *seeing* one must beckon intent" (6,15,310)
"the point of the second attention" (6,10,199)(6,13,254)
"warriors should never attempt *seeing* unless" (7,14,219)
"we fixate it by intending that fixation" (9,4,69-78)(9,8,161)
"by their mere presence" (8,4,139)(8,5,182)
"he met the Spirit" (8,2,58-59)
"others whom we might call cavemen" (10,Introduction,8)
"Warriors are divided by talent and inclination" (12,12,180)
"Every warrior should strive to practice both" (6,14,290)

Chapter 4 - *Stalking* Ourselves

"Stalking ourselves" (8,3,101)
"moving the assemblage point slowly and steadily" (7,12,187)
"practicing unusual, or unusually controlled, behavior" (8,3,102)
"a slight shift in the assemblage point" (8,3,102)
"Boredom and cynicism" (9,9,171)
"mysteries that we will never comprehend" (6,14,283)
"never enter an unfamiliar situation" (6,14,280-283&293)
"a stalker must phrase his words carefully" (8,6,258&262)
"to confront others directly" (3,Introduction,11)
"free movement of Don Juan's assemblage point" (8,6,250-262)

Chapter 5 - *Dreaming*

"the dream dreams the dreamer" (4,2,81-82)
"the struggle for survival" (4,3,100)(10,5,72)(9,1,3-4)
""wake up" in one of those real worlds" (9,3,40-41)(7,17,279)
"dreaming is a warrior's jet plane" (8,2,53)
"The first step" (3,11,142-143)
"place a friend, preferably of the opposite sex" (6,7,146)

"created what warriors refer to as your energy body" (9,2,31-32)
"changing dreams" (9,3,44)(9,4,70)
"trying to be aware of falling asleep" (9,2,23)(9,2,30)(9,2,34)(9,3,35)
"Dreams are an opening" (9,2,29-30)
"I want to see energy!" (9,9,166)
"point at an object with the little finger" (9,12,234)
"strange and threatening being that might be dangerous" (9,9,169)
"scouts from the world of inorganic beings" (9,2,29-30)(9,5,84-87)
"gives dreamers an energetic boost" (9,9,180-182)
"the dreaming emissary" (9,3,38-39)(9,4,64-68&74)
"more powerful scouts" (9,9,177-179)
"going into a war zone" (9,6,110)
"face to face with the physical body" (4,1,52)(4,2,70)
"wear a headband while sleeping" (3,12,163-164)
"touch the tip of the tongue to the roof of the mouth" (9,5,93-95)
"It is best to do dreaming late at night" (6,7,140&142)
"the area at the tip of the sternum" (6,7,140&142)
"women sit with legs crossed" (6,7,140&142)
"silent determination" (9,2,25)
"paradoxical, contradictory territory" (8,5,179)(7,8,134)(8,2,58)(8,4,143)(8,6,240)
"to wish without wishing, to do without doing" (9,2,25)

Chapter 6 - No Longer a Piece of Meat

"it leaves a furrow in the Earth's energy" (9,1,5)
"human body starts to consume itself"
Authorship unattributed. Areas of Study: Muscle Function.
   http://www.nasa.gov/exploration/humanresearch/areas_study/physiology/physiology_muscle.html
Authorship unattributed. Physiological Effects Of Weightlessness
   http://library.thinkquest.org/C003763/index.php?page=ada

pt02
Authorship unattributed. Space Bones.
   http://science.nasa.gov/science-news/science-at-nasa/2001/ast01oct_1/
Crowell, Benjamin. Biological Effects of Weightlessness.
   http://www.vias.org/physics/bk1_05_07.html
White, Ronald J. Weightlessness and the Human Body.
   http//:www.msu.edu/user/flaniga9/0998white.html

Almost all the articles written about the effects of weightlessness are from those who are space travel boosters. Consequently, the adverse effects are minimized and compared to earthly phenomena that the "lay" audience can understand, no matter how inappropriate the analogy might be. A good example is the frequent comparison of the loss of muscle mass in space travelers to the muscular atrophy that occurs in patients who are bedridden for lengthy periods. The difference, of course, is that astronauts are not immobilized or ill. They exercise several hours per day and move around performing experiments, routine maintenance and other tasks - but their muscle mass still decreases.

"to experience "God" when she so desires" (7,16,256-261)
"Those who pride themselves on being rational" (5,3,149) (7,3,49)
"intuitive, non-linear and irrational process" (8,1,34)
"To reduce an unfathomable mystery to a mathematical equation" (7,12,186)
"the mystic waiting to emerge" (8,5,188)
"the necessity of exploring our mystical side" (8,4,170)(8,6,260)

Chapter 7 - The 1960's

None

Chapter 8 - The Authenticity of Castaneda's Reportage

"Don Juan refused to fill out forms" (3,1,25)
"Since it was Don Juan's task" (8,5,206)
"Don Juan was present at a small gathering" (2,4,76)

"tyrannical, sexually obsessed control freak" Wallace, *Sorcerer's Apprentice*, Ch. 29, Pg. 242; Ch. 35, Pg. 295; Ch. 13, Pg. 110; Ch. 15, Pg. 133; Ch. 20, Pg. 175; Ch. 23, Pg. 197; Ch. 32, Pg. 267; Ch. 39, Pg. 327.
"by far the biggest indulger" (8,3,95)
"Even the author's portrait" De Mille, *The Don Juan Papers*, Pg. 531. The illustration's caption refers to "Looking and Seeing", a sarcastic reference to *"Seeing"*, a warrior's alternate method of perceiving the world around him.
"Castaneda himself was confused about the ultimate goal" (5,4,212)(5,6,315)(6,8,171)

Chapter 9 - The Transition to the Third Attention

"First Attention" (9,1,16)
"Second Attention" (9,1,16-17)
"Third Attention" (7,7,120)
"to merge with the energy outside" (7,7,120)
"all the energetic emanations inside the shell light up" (7,Epilogue,295)
"specialized, hi-speed, independent inorganic being" (10,5,104-105)
"creature such as a small insect" (5,6,313-314)
"Don Juan and Don Genaro were spotted" (6,2,46-47)
"Don Juan was seen by Florinda Donner-Grau" Wallace, *Sorcerer's Apprentice* Ch. 3, Pg. 43.
"with a movement of his head" (6,2,47)
"he would somehow let them know" (6,4,84)
"they had communicated with Eligio" (6,3,60)
"don Juan's most talented apprentice" (5,4,212)
"he joined don Juan's party" (5,4,210)(6,3,60)(6,4,87)
"vital information about the relationship" (6,3,61)

Chapter 10 - Psychoactive Plants and the Warrior's Way

"the traditional methods of moving the assemblage point" (5,5,257)
"those had parented children" (5,5,256)

"hole in the luminous energy shell" (5,3,118&120)
"result in a warrior's very real death" (9,9,178)(10,Introduction,6)
"immobilize the position of a warrior's assemblage point" (9,10,197)
"immobilize our assemblage points" (9,10,197)

Chapter 11 - Energy, Creativity and Wellness

"one cannot make the same choice" (4,11,214)
"Hunter Davies in his authorized biography" Davies, *The Beatles* Ch. 30, Pgs. 263-268
"fixation of the first attention of other people" (6,7,142)
"sick patients who are prayed for"
Authorship unattributed. Studies On Intercessory Prayer
    http://en.wikipedia.org/wiki/Studies_on_intercessory_prayer
Brower, Anne. Do Prayer Studies Work?
http://newsweek.washingtonpost.com/
    onfaith/faithandhealing/2009/04/the_power_of_prayer
"can guarantee a healthy existence" (5,5,236)(10,1,16-17)
"uses up too much energy" (8,3,92)
"variety and fluidity of their internal dialogue" (7,9,158)
"to tell himself the opposite" (3,15,239)
"warriors avoid confronting others bluntly" (3,Introduction,11)
"no one is doing anything to anyone" (3,11,138-139)

Chapter 12 - The Conditions of Modern Life

"unbending intent" (8,2,62)(1,1,84)(1,1,149)(1,1,152)

Chapter 13 - The Misunderstanding

"heightened awareness" (7,1,23-34)(9,1,17)(9,3,51)
"Don Juan tailored his instruction" (11,2,23-34)(7,1,17)
"The Rule Of The Nagual" (6,9,176-181)
"an apprentice' long term goal" (8,Introduction,17)(9,Author's

Note,xi)(6,9,176-181)

Chapter 14 - The Flyers

"alien intelligence" (12,15,218-225)
"we have two minds" (12,15,218-225)
"The Warrior's Way is a prescription for action" (2,5,106-107)
"the only real advantage of having a teacher" (8,15,178)
(8,6,270)
"impeccable men and women need no one to guide them" (7,11,178)
"without the intervention of the Spirit" (7,15,237)(8,3,99)
(12,Introduction,9-10)
"become the prisoner of other awareness " (9,10,197)

Chapter 15 - The Sexual Obsession

"You make your own luck" (3,18,278)(2,12,220)
"intending in the second attention" (9,12,231-232)
"our awareness of time is altered" (7,18,288-289)

Chapter 16 - Evil

"Warriors don't accept evil" (8,6,284)
"the reason for the gift of life is the enhancement of consciousness" (7,3,50-51)

Chapter 17 - The Beginnings of the Warrior's Way

"energetic descendants of the ancient Toltecs" (5,4,180-181)(6,1,20)(7,1,17)
"they started on the path to knowledge" (7,1,17)
"a gradual split developed among them" (6,1,23)(7,1,15-19)(7,11,170)
"accumulate power over their fellow men" (6,1,28)(7,1,15)(9,11,203&206)
"the seekers of total freedom" (7,Foreword,13)
"the old seers left behind many artifacts" (6,1,15-26)

"scare them to death" (7,15,245)(7,6,111)
"Certain geographical areas" (7,9,146&152)
"seers who wish to adopt animal forms" (7,9,146)

Chapter 18 - Inorganic Beings

"one of the strangest phenomena presented to us" (9,5,83)
"a world of their own" (9,5,88&100)(9,9,179)(10,5,104)(9,6,108)
"were left to roam aimlessly" (5,3,164)
"inorganic beings take on whatever form" (5,3,151-152)(12,13,199)
"they sometimes move among us" (2,2,52-58)
"accounted for the existence of inorganic beings" (7,10,162)
"a sleeping bag with a small zipper" (7,18,287)
"the extraordinarily long duration" (7,15,232)
"the rolling force" (7,14,224-228)
"the rolling force is hitting harder" (7,14,228)
"only with their cooperation" (9,9,179)
"huge dark brown mass" (9,5,88)
"pressed together as long hollow tubes" (9,5,89&100)
"the labyrinth of penumbra" (9,5,100)
"thick yellow, fog-like vapors everywhere" (9,7,133)
"inorganic beings roam that plain" (6,8,159-162)
"There are two kinds of inorganic beings" (7,6,109)
"seek the high-energy aura of *dreamers*" (9,6,107)(9,6,115)
"send their scouts into our dreams" (9,5,84-89)
"fewer in number but more noticeable" (9,5,85)
"A *dreamer* must be the one to first initiate contact" (9,5,87)(9,3,45-49)
"teach secrets of manipulating awareness" (9,5,90)
"*dreamer's* most secret weaknesses and obsessions" (9,7,137)(9,5,96)(6,1,57)
"for nearly an eternity" (9,9,180)
"re-structure his energy shape to closely resemble theirs" (7,15,231-232)
"gain power and control" (6,1,25-26)
"transform himself into any other living thing"(6,1,55)

"has the energy to recreate" (1,10,140)
"witness distant realms" (9,2,29-30)(9,3,45-49)
"meet awareness from worlds unknown to us" (9,6,119)
"But the price for these favors is enslavement" (9,4,66)(9,5,96-97)
"perception of that world the only possible one" (9,10,196-197)
"the quirks of *dreamer's* personality" (9,7,137)
"discharges all of the *dreamer's* energy" (9,7,132)
"resulting in death" (9,7,131-132)
"The universe of the inorganic beings is female" (9,10,188)
"There are two examples" (9,5,102-105)(9,10,190-197)
"move in and out of that world at will" (9,10,187-188)
"gives her a energy boost" (9,9,180-182)
"given to them by their benefactor" (7,6,112)
"lurking around menacingly" (5,3,139-147)
"come into physical contact with one" (7,7,113)
"animal fear" (7,6,110)
"doling out their energy in short bursts of fear" (7,6,110-111)
"made one of his allies materialize itself" (7,6,112)
"Castaneda saw don Juan and don Genaro's allies as" (5,3,139-140)
"used one to guard his house" (7,7,113)
"Castaneda felt a threatening presence" (2,14,243)
"keep a wayward apprentice in line" (5,1,52-55)
"impeccable and detached nagual" (7,6,109)
"Castaneda quoted don Juan" (1,3,38)(1,7,104&110)
"make contact with inorganic beings" (2,2,52-53)
"first face-to-face contact" (2,13,224)(2,15,271)

Chapter 19 - Why the Warrior's Way? And Why Now?

"evolve much faster than physical evolution can occur" (10,5,104)
"people love to be told what to do" (5,5,222)
"All of them must be practiced tirelessly" (9,3,37)

Chapter 20 - The Life of Don Juan Matus

"born in Yuma, Arizona" (10,Introduction,1)
"1891" (1,Introduction,5)
"His father was a Yaqui Indian from Sonora, Mexico" (10,Introduction,1)
"Yuma Indian from Arizona" (10,Introduction,1)
"Battle of El Anil in 1886" Authorship unattributed. Yaqui Wars. http://en.wikipedia.org/wiki/Yaqui_Wars
"don Juan's family returned to Sonora" (10,Introduction,1)
"Mexican soldiers came upon their camp" (2,9,166-168)
"tobacco plantations of Yucatan" (6,9,175-176)
"constant threat of starvation" (2,3,61)
"Before his father's death don Juan had promised him" (2,9,175)
"mean and wild young man" (6,9,175-176)(8,3,74-75)
"hated the humble attitude" (4,1,27)
"he was working in a sugar mill" (7,2,33-42)
"old man who had prevented don Juan's certain death" (7,2,33-42)
"three omens" (8,1,32-33)
"Realizing that he had to act fast" (7,12,190-202)
"Belisario and his wife were packing their things" (8,3,74-88)
"the old man took don Juan to a large hacienda" (8,5,192-215)
"I didn't know that I was storing power" (3,14,214)
"the beautiful women of his party" (11,2,24-25)
"to confront the monstrous man" (8,5,192-215)
"Naguals are not really the most friendly beings on earth" (9,11,202)
"taught by two opposite temperaments" (8,1,28)
"nagual Julian was not given to explanations" (7,7,116)
"nagual Julian was loud and extroverted" (12,4,71)
"for which he felt very guilty" (8,2,54)
"His dramas were always bigger than life" (7,12,202)
"The apprentices nearly died there" (7,4,70)
"don Juan's failure to follow directions" (6,1,31-32)
"After securing don Juan as his apprentice" (6,9,184-190)
"Vicente, the nagual Julian's first apprentice" (6,11,215) (8,3,94)
"They both sold plants and potions" (2,2,42)

"the nagual promised to give him a lesson" (8,6,250-262)
"male nagual's counterpart and soul mate" (6,6,127)
"nagual Julian did find a nagual woman" (6,11,216-221)
"don Juan was an expert" (1,Introduction,7)
"herbal mixture containing the psychoactive mushroom" (2,8,161)
"strange, almost supernatural vigor" (1,3,48)
"The devil's weed nearly killed me" (1,5,82)
"My benefactor was given to shouting" (1,10,138)
"Jimson weed and the mushroom mixture" (1,Introduction,7)
"He had don Juan build a mirror" (7,6,106-112)
"materialize themselves in this world" (9,3,48)(7,6,112)(7,7,113)
"don Juan found them repulsive" (9,9,180-182)
"he used one of them to guard his house" (7,7,113)
"invested the money in stocks and bonds" (4,2,161-162)
"developed a love for reading" (8,6,251)
"He could speak superb Spanish" (2,Introduction,14)
"sophisticated urban dweller" (4,2,106)
"He regularly went to Mexico City" (9,10,184)(7,3,51)
"1960" (3,1,19)
"He set up four different households" (6,10,211)
"somewhere in the mountainous region near Oaxaca" (12,18,215)
"very modest dwelling in Sonora" (12,16,187)
"Greyhound bus station in Nogales, Arizona" (1,Introduction,1)(12,1,38)
"five feet nine inches tall" (12,4,67)(2,Introduction,10)
"The secret is not in what you do" (3,14,195)
"He drank only water" (8,3,92)(2,4,84)(2,4,90)
"He sometimes chewed peyote buttons" (2,3,69)
"disagreed with his teaching method" (6,9,184-185)
"he was nearly seventy years old" (1,Introduction,5)(3,1,19)
"He strongly empathized" (8,6,246-247)
"What you're witnessing is the result of a lifelong struggle" (8,6,247)
"He also appreciated the fact" (7,15,246)
"on an abrupt note" (2,Introduction,17)

"their relationship with the death defier" (9,11,213-215)
"He first came into contact with the nagual Sebastian" (9,4,60-63)
"The death defier had learned to manipulate" (7,15,252-253)
"knowledge necessary for a nagual to attain total perception" (9,11,217)
"how to become a woman" (9,11,213-215)
"the twin positions" (9,12,229-230&232)
"The nagual Julian knew that this was to be don Juan's task" (8,5,206)
"He found six other apprentices" (5,1,51-58)(6,11,223-231)
"Don Juan found her" (6,11,223-231)
"The nagual woman carried books of poetry" (6,6,127)
"He generally only enjoyed" (6,2,44)
"Don Juan spent hours looking at mundane, trivial things" (7,17,268)
"His last moments in this world" (6,15,315-316)

Chapter 21 - A Summary of Practical Applications of the Warrior's Way

"The position of a child's assemblage point" (7,8,137-138&143)
"A fluid and varied internal dialogue is essential" (7,9,158)
"One method is to roll the eyes in a circular motion" (7,16,258)
"Another method for men" (6,7,140&142)
"concentrate on the exact midpoint of the body" (7,7,114)
"If any one of these actions is removed" (5,5,222)
"He even recommended that we seek them out" (7,2,29-33)
"those seemingly most active in helping others" (7,12,188)
"never carry anything is his hands" (3,3,38)
"always stretch the entire body" (9,11,204)
"sleep sitting up in a comfortable chair" (8,2,45)
"taking naps while lying on the stomach" (8,2,45-46)
"For an energy boost" (5,5,267-268)
"the cause of meanness in adults" (2,9,168)

Chapter 22 - The Moment of Revelation

"master manipulators of perception" (7,8,138)(10,3,37-38)
"we are all *seeing* energy" (10,5,129)

Appendix II - Deleted section of Ch. 8 - The Authenticity of Castaneda's Reportage

"He was saving you for something" (5,5,229)
"Don Juan had to concoct an elaborate tale" (6,12,233-234)
"the real power behind the throne" (6,2,150)
"It was Don Juan who first suggested that Castaneda write a book" (6,1,27)(8,Introduction,13-14)
"He also encouraged Castaneda to think of him as a sorcerer" (7,1,17)
"Castaneda's companion at his first meeting" (12,2,32)
"Castaneda feared Don Juan more than death" (3,4,27)(7,4,59)
"Don Juan warned Castaneda, in a surreptitious manner" (7,12,195)
"He told me that your spirit takes prisoners" (5,1,57)

Appendix III - The Return of the Nagual Woman

"Don Juan and the old seer" (9,12,234)
"Don Juan resented being forced" (9,13,255)(9,11,213)
"all the naguals of don Juan's lineage" (9,11,214)(9,4,62)(8,3,78)
"ruthless and self-indulgent old seers" (9,11,203&205)
"cultivated for thousands of years" (9,11,207)
"intended in the Second Attention" (9,12,231-232)
"an exact replica of a small town" (9,11,203)
"To intend this dream world forward" (9,13,254&258)
"extracted a large amount from Castaneda" (9,12,239)(9,13,251&255)
"merging his awareness with" (9,13,258); Carol Tiggs, Speech at Tensegrity Workshop, Oct. 8, 1995, Culver City CA.; Carol Tiggs, Speech on Cleargreen Field Trip, May 22(?), 1995, Tula, Mexico.
"inexperience and naivety" (9,10,190-195); Carol Tiggs, Speech on Cleargreen Field Trip, May 22(?), 1995, Tula,

Mexico; Wallace, *Sorcerer's Apprentice*, Ch. 18, Pgs. 155-159.
"fixate the awareness of the entire group" (9,10,196-197)
"The death defier did not seek" (7,15,253)(9,11,215)
"sought the freedom to indulge his eccentricities" (9,11,215)
"a broken woman, her energy sapped" Wallace, *Sorcerer's Apprentice*, Ch. 18, Pg. 159.
"mere pawn in Castaneda's group of followers" Wallace, *Sorcerer's Apprentice*, Ch. 36, Pg. 312 & Ch. 37, Pg. 315.
"which only inorganic beings have" (9,5,100)
"They did this together once" (6,2,46-47)
"don Juan did it by himself another time" Wallace, *Sorcerer's Apprentice*, Ch. 3, Pg. 43.
"don Juan's most powerful apprentice, Eligio" (6,12,241)(5,4,212)
"attach himself to don Juan's party" (6,12,241)
"communicated with two of don Juan's apprentices" (6,3,60)
"were shocked to the core" Castaneda, Interviewed by Bruce Wagner in *Details* magazine, March 1994;Wallace, *Sorcerer's Apprentice*, Ch. 18, Pg. 159.
"stuck in the Second Attention" Wallace, *Sorcerer's Apprentice*, Ch. 6, Pg. 63.
"egomaniacal obsessions" Wallace, *Sorcerer's Apprentice*, Ch. 13, Pg. 111.
"walked right by him" Wallace, *Sorcerer's Apprentice*, Ch. 3, Pg. 43.
"claimed that she had no memory" Carol Tiggs, Speech at Tensegrity Workshop, Oct. 8, 1995, Culver City CA, sustainedaction.org; Wallace, *Sorcerer's Apprentice*, Ch. 3, Pg. 44. *(The Sustained Action website began as an attempt by some of Castaneda's most devoted followers to make sense of their experiences within the group. Thoughtful and reasoned discussion, however, soon degenerated into an orgy of self-loathing and doubt. Crude insult replaced any semblance of civility. By the time that Sustained Action morphed into the Sustained Reaction discussion group, the level of discourse had sunk to a grade-school level among anonymous individuals. Assertions and accusations by those who refuse to identify themselves mean <u>nothing</u>. Some of the posts have been very long*

and involved efforts to add to the chorus of skeptics screaming for Castaneda's head on a stick, but their "scholarship" seldom includes the precise attribution of sources required to convince anyone but fellow cynics.)

"stash some money" Carol Tiggs, Speech at Tensegrity Workshop, May 19, 1995 Mexico City, Mexico sustainedaction.org; Wallace, *Sorcerer's Apprentice*, Ch. 3, Pg. 44.
"foreshadowing of the nagual woman's fate" (6,6,128)
"has done searches of public records" Jennings (Donovan), Carol Tiggs Chronology Pts. 1-7, sustainedaction.org
"nagual woman left with don Juan's party in 1973" (6,15,313-314)(10,Introduction,6)(9,11,204)
"get on with her life" Jennings (Donovan), Carol Tiggs Chronology Pts. 1-7, sustainedaction.org
"never left in the first place" Wallace, *Sorcerer's Apprentice*, Ch. 29, Pg. 243 & Appendix A, Pg. 407.
"having lived an ordinary life" Wallace, *Sorcerer's Apprentice*, Ch. 47, Pg. 389.
"which was available when she wrote her book" Jennings (Donovan), Carol Tiggs Chronology Pts. 1-7, sustainedaction.org
"Wallace was a witness" Wallace, *Sorcerer's Apprentice*, Ch. 36, Pg. 312.
"merely fallen from favor" Wallace, *Sorcerer's Apprentice*, Ch. 29, Pg. 243.
"greeted with such fanfare" Castaneda, Interviewed by Bruce Wagner in Details magazine, March 1994;Wallace, *Sorcerer's Apprentice*, Ch. 18, Pg. 159; Donner-Grau, Tensegrity Workshop, Maui HI, March 24-26, 1995, sustainedaction.org; Castaneda, Lecture at Tensegrity Workshop, Culver City CA, Aug. 1995, sustainedaction.org; Hammond, "Carlos Castaneda's Tensegrity", *Yoga Journal*, Dec. 1995; Castaneda, Lecture at Tensegrity Workshop, UCLA, Westwood, CA, Mar. 1-3, 1996, sustainedaction.org; Epstein, "My Lunch with Carlos Castaneda", *Psychology Today*, March/April 1996.
"woman whom Wallace referred to" Wallace, *Sorcerer's*

Apprentice, Ch. 29, Pg. 243.
"major financial participation" Jennings (Donovan), Carol Tiggs Chronology Pts. 4-6, sustainedaction.org; Wallace, *Sorcerer's Apprentice*, Appendix A, Pg. 408.
"1)" (7,6,87)
"2)" (7,7,120)(12,13,192)(10,5,104)
"3)" (9,1,16-17)(7,7,120)(12,13,192)
"4)" (8,6,224)
"5)" (1,10,132-133)(7,9,156)
"6)" (6,3,61-62)(6,4,88)(6,5,110)
"7)" (6,15,309-310)
"8)" (2,5,112-113)
"9)" (6,10,198-199)(6,15,312)(7,Foreword,11)(1,2,23-32)
"10)" (9,7,137-138)
"11)" (6,14,287-292)(8,4,145)(9,8,147-148&150)(10,5,108)(11,6,220-221)(12,10,142-149&158)
"12)" (7,13,215)(7,7,120)(7,Epilogue,295)
"13)" Donner, Being-In-Dreaming, Ch. 4, Pg. 61; Ch. 7, Pg. 110.
"14)" Non-existent passages cannot be cited.
"15)" (8,1,34-44)(8,5,200)
"16)" Jennings (Donovan), Blue Scout Chronology Pts. 1-5, sustainedaction.org

Appendix IV - The Blue Scout

"Blue Scout made her first (and only) appearance" (9,6,120-121)
"float in and out of rooms like ghosts" (9,7,134-135)
"woman originally named Patty Partin" Jennings, Blue Scout Chronology, Pts. I-VI, sustainedaction.org
"the unpleasant task of weeding out" Wallace, *Sorcerer's Apprentice*, Appendix A, Pg. 409.
"a back story was created for her" Wallace, *Sorcerer's Apprentice*, Appendix A, Pg. 408.
"having sex could lead to his downfall" Castaneda, *A Journal Of Applied Hermeneutics*, "The Warrior's Way as a Philosophical-Practical Paradigm", Pt. 2.

"that he could lose his mind" (8,2,55-56)
"He feared don Juan" (7,4,59)
"even from the Third Attention" (6,2,46-47)
"sidetracked by the Death Defier" (9,13,257-258)
"Having grown disgusted with Castaneda" Wallace, *Sorcerer's Apprentice*, Ch. 2, Pgs. 32-33.
"she tried to take Florinda Donner-Grau" Jennings, Florinda Donner-Grau
    Chronology, Pt. III, sustainedaction.org.
"who had remained behind" (6,15,308)(11,5,179)
"She departed for the Third Attention" Wallace, *Sorcerer's Apprentice*, Ch. 13, Pg. 111.

Appendix V - Debunking De Mille

Castaneda's Journey

"If I were a struggling graduate student" De Mille, *Castaneda's Journey*, Ch. 1, Pg. 18.
"Carlos first heard about *seeing* six years after he first *saw*" De Mille, *Castaneda's Journey*, Ch. 3, Pg. 37.
"the events of Jan. 29, 1962" (3,13,182)
"the conversation of May 21, 1968" (2,2,36)
"sometime before May 14, 1962" (2,Introduction,20-21)
"de Mille asserts that sewing the eyelids" De Mille, *Castaneda's Journey*, Ch. 3, Pgs. 41-43.
"The directions given by don Juan for sewing" (1,5,86)
"exactly how Castaneda described it" (1,9,123)
"Wasson's concerns about Castaneda's work" De Mille, *Castaneda's Journey*, Ch. 3, Pgs. 43-47.
"He replied fully and intelligently" Wasson, Review of *Journey To Ixtlan*, *Economic Botany*, Jan.-Mar. 1973, Pgs. 151-152.
"Subject to refutation by long-awaited proofs" De Mille, *Castaneda's Journey*, Ch. 3, Pg. 51.
"poor pilgrim lost on his way" De Mille, *Castaneda's Journey*, Ch. 3, Pg. 47.
"The complete quote from Wasson's review" Wasson, Review of *Journey To Ixtlan*, *Economic Botany*, Jan.-Mar. 1973, Pgs.

151-152.
"letter that de Mille himself admits" De Mille, *The Don Juan Papers*, Ch. 13, Pg. 126.
"Goldschmidt filed a formal complaint" De Mille, *The Don Juan Papers*, Ch. 13, Pg. 127.
"Goldschmidt did indeed become cowed" Goldschmidt, "The Pleasure Principle", Interviewed by Mark Ehrman, *Los Angeles Times*, Nov. 20, 2005.
"five faculty members signed" De Mille, *Castaneda's Journey*, Ch. 4, Pg. 68.
"his truth as a witness is not in question" De Mille, *Castaneda's Journey*, Ch. 4, Pg. 64.
"human body when seen as pure energy" De Mille, *Castaneda's Journey*, Ch. 5, Pg. 94.
"many other common perceptions" Harner, Letter, *New York Times Book Review*, May 7, 1978.
"comparison of anthropologist Peter Furst's account" *Castaneda's Journey*, Ch. 6, Pgs. 112-113.
"Castaneda's account of don Genaro" (2,6, 124-128)
"Silva was leaping from rock to rock" Furst, *Rock Crystals and Peyote Dreams*, Ch. 2.
"wearing a large, showy costume"
http://sustainedaction.org/Images_Photos/
    ramon_medina_silva_waterfall.htm
"recounts his conversations with another witness" De Mille, *The Don Juan Papers*, Ch. 42,Pgs. 339-354.
"Myerhoff was very unsure of the chronology" De Mille, *The Don Juan Papers*, Notes, Pg. 486.
"Myerhoff and Castaneda were UCLA students" De Mille, *The Don Juan Papers*, Ch. 42,Pg. 336.
"defended her dissertation" De Mille, *The Don Juan Papers*, Ch. 42, Pg. 338.
"1970 series of lectures at UCLA" De Mille, *The Don Juan Papers*, Ch. 42,Pg. 338.
"nothing else to say on the subject" De Mille, *Castaneda's Journey*, Ch. 6, Pg. 113.
"demonstration was like don Genaro's is suspect" De Mille, *The Don Juan Papers*, Ch. 42, Pg. 338.

"what the terms tonal and nagual mean" De Mille, *Castaneda's Journey*, Ch. 7, Pgs. 117-128.
"another alleged discrepancy" De Mille, *Castaneda's Journey*, Pg. 168.
"I wanted to ask what I was supposed to see" (3,12,157)
"de Mille makes much of Castaneda's 1965 encounter" De Mille, *Castaneda's Journey*, Pgs. 170-171.
"Castaneda believes it to be a female" (1,11,147-148)
"spread throughout *Castaneda's Journey*" De Mille, *Castaneda's Journey*, Pg. 171, Pg. 160, Pg. 137, Pg. 135, Pg. 128, Pg. 121, Pg. 96, Pg. 93, Pg.75, Pgs. 70-71, Pg. 66, Pgs. 62-63, Pg. 58.
"Castaneda had to "experience" all of the events chronicled" De Mille, *Castaneda's Journey*, Pgs. 171-172.
"dissatisfaction with Castaneda's translations" De Mille, *Castaneda's Journey*, Pgs. 172-176.

The Don Juan Papers

"Carlos meets a certain witch named La Catalina" De Mille, *The Don Juan Papers*, Ch. 2,Pg. 18.
"Castaneda did not know the identity" (1,11,145-148)
"unaccountably he has never heard of it in 1968" De Mille, *The Don Juan Papers*, Ch. 2,Pg. 18.
"Don Juan had referred to *seeing* briefly" (3,12,157)(3,13,182)
"The most detailed conversation about *seeing*" (2,Introduction,20-21)
"His statements sounded like gibberish to me" (2,Introduction,24)
"Castaneda did not begin to understand" (2,2,49-53)
"brief conversation about seeing on May 21, 1968" (2,2,36)
"*The Teachings* tells a gothic tale full of fear" De Mille, *The Don Juan Papers*, Ch. 2,Pg. 18.
"there are over a dozen examples" (1,2,30)(1,2,31)(1,2,33)(1,2,37)(1,3,44)(1,3,47) (1,6,100)(1,6,101)(1,7,103)(1,8,119)(1,8,121)(1,10,130)(1,11,148)
"second kind of proof" De Mille, *The Don Juan Papers*, Ch. 2,Pg. 19.

"Since I was capable of writing down most of what was said" (3,Introduction,8)
"With prodigious speed and skill" De Mille, *The Don Juan Papers*, Ch. 2,Pg. 19.
"Jose Cuellar, described his ability as" Cuellar, *Boulder Magazine*, Apr.-May 1978, Pg. 23.
"No one but Castaneda has seen don Juan" De Mille, *The Don Juan Papers*, Ch. 2,Pg. 19.
"identified as William Laurence Campbell" Wanderling, Don Juan Matus: Real Or Imagined?, http://www.the-wanderling.com/don_juan.html#N3000
"believed him to be Alan Morrison" Castaneda, *A Magical Journey with Carlos Castaneda*, Ch. 15, Pg. 103.
"spoken to don Juan on at least one other occasion" (12,1,40)
"Castaneda and don Juan were pursued" (4,7,147)
"a man de Mille praises and derides" De Mille, *The Don Juan Papers*, Ch. 6, Pgs. 61-62, Ch. 6, Pg. 45.
"de Mille mentions two others" De Mille, *The Don Juan Papers*, Notes, Pg. 440.
"a matter of inter-departmental conflict" Cuellar, *Boulder Magazine*, Apr.-May 1978, Pgs. 21-22.
"Castaneda himself confirmed this in a letter" Castaneda, *A Magical Journey with Carlos Castaneda*, Ch. 20, Pg. 139.
"there was no presentation " De Mille, *The Don Juan Papers*, Ch. 2, Pg. 19.
"accusation that there were no actual field notes" Castaneda, *A Magical Journey with Carlos Castaneda*, Ch. 18, Pg. 128.
"He did not disclose his shaman's residence" Beals, *American Anthropologist*, June 1978, Pg. 357.
"He had handfuls of incompletes" Interview, De Mille, *The Don Juan Papers*, Ch. 42, Pg. 351.
"Castaneda did actually drop out of UCLA in 1965" Castaneda, *A Magical Journey with Carlos Castaneda*, Ch. 18, Pg. 129.
"de Mille hypothesis that any field notes extant" De Mille, *The Don Juan Papers*, Ch. 2, Pg. 19.
"third kind of proof" De Mille, *The Don Juan Papers*, Ch. 2, Pg. 19.

"De Mille's second example is a severely edited quotation" De Mille, *The Don Juan Papers*, Ch. 2, Pg. 20.
"article that appeared in *Psychedelic Review*" Swain et al, *Psychedelic Review*, Fall 1963, Pgs. 219-243.
"Then de Mille abstracts another quotation" De Mille, *The Don Juan Papers*, Ch. 2, Pg. 20.
"Castaneda's first experience with datura" (1,3,44-45)
"de Mille's analysis of these two passages" De Mille, *The Don Juan Papers*, Ch. 2, Pg. 20.
"nobody had actually tried to smoke them" De Mille, *The Don Juan Papers*, Ch. 2, Pg. 23.
"Castaneda described the procedure" (2,Introduction,15)
"One of the sources that de Mille listed" Pollock, "The Psilocybin Mushroom Pandemic", *Journal of Psychedelic Drugs*, Jan.-Mar. 1975, Pgs. 73-84.
"As noted by Anton Koote" Koote, "A Critical Look At Castaneda's Critics", *The Journal Of Mind And Behavior*, 1984, 5, Pgs. 99-108.
"Castaneda's critics want to have it both ways" Ibid.
"don Juan and Castaneda stalked rabbits bare-handed" De Mille, *The Don Juan Papers*, Ch. 6, Pg. 57.
"used traps assembled from materials" (3,7,83)(3,8,96-97)(3,8,100)(3,9,113)
"Don Juan was educated" (8,12,200-201)
"some of whom came from the same well-educated background" (8,1,38)
"from which the nagual Julian himself emerged" (8,2,63)
"The household's wealth gave them access" (8,6,252)

Contemporaneous Witnesses

Margaret Runyan Castaneda 1): Interview, De Mille, *Castaneda's Journey*, Ch. 3, Pg. 58.
Margaret Runyan Castaneda 2): Castaneda, *A Magical Journey with Carlos Castaneda*, Ch. 15, Pg. 115.
Dr. C. Scott Littleton 1) Letter to Laura Knight-Jadczyk, *Adventures With Cassiopaea*, Ch. 42.,
http://cassiopaea.org/2011/11/26/the-wave-chapter-42-

the-tradition/
"Castaneda had a habit of referring" (8,Introduction,16)
Dr. C. Scott Littleton 2): Littleton, *Journal Of Latin American Lore*, 1976, Vol. 2, No. 2, Pgs. 145-155.
Dr. C. Scott Littleton 3) E-mail to Dr. Jack Starfatti, June 30, 2001
Dr. Jose Cuellar: Interview, *Boulder Magazine*, Apr.-May 1978, Pgs. 22-23.
Dr. Ralph Beals: Beals, *American Anthropologist*, June 1978, Pgs. 357 & 359.
Dr. Barbara Myerhoff: Interview, De Mille, *The Don Juan Papers*, Ch. 42, Pgs. 339-354.
Dr. Clement Meighan: Castaneda, *A Magical Journey with Carlos Castaneda*, Ch. 19, Pgs. 140-141.
Michael Harner: Letter to the Editor, *New York Times Book Review*, May 7, 1978, Pg. 45.
"Robert Bly in his review" Bly, *New York Times Book Review*, Jan. 22, 1978, Pg. 22.
"to assert that these questions discredit" De Mille, *The Don Juan Papers*, Ch. 2, Pg. 22.

Bibliography

Books

Castaneda, Carlos. *The Teachings of Don Juan : A Yaqui Way of Knowledge* (30th Anniversary Edition). Los Angeles and Berkeley, California. The University of California Press, 1998.
Castaneda, Carlos. *A Separate Reality*. New York : Simon And Schuster, 1971.
Castaneda, Carlos. *Journey to Ixtlan*. New York : Simon And Schuster, 1972.
Castaneda, Carlos. *Tales of Power*. New York : Simon And Schuster, 1974.
Castaneda, Carlos. *The Second Ring of Power*. New York : Simon And Schuster, 1977.
Castaneda, Carlos. *The Eagle's Gift*. New York : Simon And Schuster, 1981.
Castaneda, Carlos. *The Fire From Within*. New York : Simon And Schuster, 1984.
Castaneda, Carlos. *The Power of Silence*. New York : Simon And Schuster, 1987.
Castaneda, Carlos. *The Art of Dreaming*. New York : HarperCollins, 1993.
Castaneda, Carlos. *Magical Passes*. New York : HarperCollins, 1998.
Castaneda, Carlos. *The Wheel of Time*. Los Angeles : LA Eidolona Press, 1998.
Castaneda, Carlos. *The Active Side of Infinity*. New York : HarperCollins, 1998.
Castaneda, Carlos. *A Journal of Applied Hermeneutics*. Vol. 1, Nos. 1-4, 1996.
Castaneda, Margaret Runyan. *A Magical Journey with Carlos Castaneda*. iUniverse.com, Inc., 2001. (Paperback)
Davies, Hunter. *The Beatles*. New York: McGraw-Hill, 1978 (1st revised edition)
De Mille, Richard. *Castaneda's Journey*. Santa Barbara, California. Capra Press, 1976. (Paperback)(Identical to the 2001 revised version)

De Mille, Richard. *The Don Juan Papers.* iUniverse.com, Inc., 2001. (Revised Edition) (Paperback)
Donner, Florinda. *Being-In-Dreaming.* New York : HarperCollins, 1991. (Paperback)
Furst, Peter. The Chasm Between The Worlds. *Rock Crystals and Peyote Dreams*, University of Utah Press, 2006, Ch. 2 with Afterword, http://petertfurst.com/ [*This excerpt from Furst's book contains several pictures of Ramon Medina Silva's "waterfall jumping."*]
Wallace, Amy. *Sorcerer's Apprentice.* Berkeley, California. Frog, Ltd., 2003.

Articles

Authorship unattributed. Areas of Study: Muscle Function. http://www.nasa.gov/exploration/humanresearch/areas_study/physiology/physiology_muscle.html
Authorship unattributed. Physiological Effects Of Weightlessness. http://library.thinkquest.org/C003763/index.php?page=adapt02
Authorship unattributed. Space Bones. http://science.nasa.gov/science-news/science-at nasa/2001/ast01oct_1/
Authorship unattributed. Studies On Intercessory Prayer. http://en.wikipedia.org/wiki/Studies_on_intercessory_prayer
Authorship unattributed. Yaqui Wars. http://en.wikipedia.org/wiki/Yaqui_Wars
Beals, Ralph L.. Sonoran Fantasy or Coming of Age. *American Anthropologist*, June 1978, Vol. 80, No. 2, Pgs. 355-362.
Brower, Anne. Do Prayer Studies Work? http://newsweek.washingtonpost.com/onfaith/faithandhealing/2009/04/the_power_of_prayer
Crowell, Benjamin. Biological Effects of Weightlessness. http://www.vias.org/physics/bk1_05_07.html
Cuellar, Jose. Interview by Michael and Patrick McNierney. *Boulder Magazine*, Vol. 1, No. 3, April-May 1978, Pgs. 20-23 &

30.
Epstein, Benjamin. My Lunch with Carlos Castaneda. *Psychology Today*, March/April 1996.
Goldschmidt, Walter. Goldschmidt, "The Pleasure Principle", Interviewed by Mark Ehrman, *Los Angeles Times*, Nov. 20, 2005.
Hammond, Holly. Carlos Castaneda's Tensegrity. *Yoga Journal*, Dec. 1995.
Harner, Michael. Letter to the Editor. *New York Times Book Review*, May 7, 1978, Pg. 45.
Jennings, Richard (Donovan, Corey). Carol Tiggs Chronology Pts. 1-7, sustainedaction.org
Jennings, Richard (Donovan, Corey). Blue Scout Chronology Pts. 1-5, sustainedaction.org
Jennings, Richard (Donovan, Corey). Florinda Donner-Grau Chronology Pts. 1-12, sustainedaction.org
Koote, Anton F., A Critical Look at Castaneda's Critics. *The Journal of Mind and Behavior*, Vol. 5, No. 1, Winter 1984, Pgs. 99-108. [*Koote's article, de Mille's response and Koote's reply are posted at* http://ttzlibrary.yuku.com/topic/587/A-Critical-Look-At-Castaneda-s-Critics-by-Anton-F-Koote]
Littleton, C. Scott. E-mail to Dr. Jack Starfatti, June 30, 2001, http://wanderling. tripod.com/littleton.html
Littleton, C. Scott. An Emic Account of Sorcery: Carlos Castaneda and the Rise of a New Anthropology. *Journal of Latin American Lore*, Vol. 2, No. 2, 1976.
Littleton, C. Scott. Letter to Laura Knight-Jadczyk, *Adventures with Cassiopaea*, Ch. 42., http://cassiopaea.org/2011/11/26/the-wave-chapter-42-the-tradition/
Pollock, Steven Hayden. The Psilocybin Mushroom Pandemic. *Journal of Psychedelic Drugs*, Vol. 7, No. 1, Jan.-Mar. 1975, Pgs. 73-84.
Silva, Ramon Medina. Photo at waterfall by Peter Furst, http://sustainedaction.org/
   Images_Photos/ramon_medina_silva_waterfall.htm
Swain, Frederic et al. Four Psilocybin Experiences. *The Psychedelic Review*, Vol. 1, No. 2, Fall 1963, Pgs. 219-243.

Wagner, Bruce. You Only Live Twice. *Details* (magazine), March 1994.
Wanderling, The. Don Juan Matus: Real Or Imagined?, http://www.the-wanderling.com/don_juan.html#N3000
Wasson, Gordon. Review of *Journey to Ixtlan*, *Economic Botany*, Vol. 27, No. 1, Jan.-Mar. 1973, Pgs. 151-152.
White, Ronald J. Weightlessness and the Human Body. http//:www.msu.edu/user/flaniga9/0998white.html

"Impeccable men need no one to guide them, that by themselves, through saving their energy, they can do everything that seers do. All they need is a minimal chance, just to be cognizant of the possibilities that seers have unraveled." (7,11,178)

"Impeccability is simply the best use of our energy level." (8,6,248)

"A man is defeated only when he no longer tries, and abandons himself." (1,3,64)

"Our link is with the spirit itself and only incidentally with the man who brings us its message." (9,1,11)

"Put your trust in yourself, not in me."(2,5,110)

Printed in Great Britain
by Amazon